Ten Great Therapy Groups

Substance Abuse and Mental Health Therapy Group Curriculum in an Easy-to-Follow Workbook Format

By Kristen Brown, LCSW

All words by Kristen Brown

Created in Virginia, Printed in the United States

Find out more at www.kbrowntherapy.com

For all the therapists, groups facilitators, and healers out there doing their best to help clients.

In the words of Tricia: be the best you can be.

Contents

Introduction

I wish that this workbook existed ten years ago. I graduated from my Master of Social Work program in 2012, and spent the next seven years in a grueling residency process. My residency was somewhat unusual as I moved overseas to England for four years right in the middle of it. I began my residency in America working in a substance abuse rehabilitation program for one year. In the UK, I logged an additional five years as a therapist for substance abuse treatment. I returned to America in 2017, and continued my residency working within inpatient and outpatient treatment centers. I finally became a Licensed Clinical Social Worker in 2019.

I used to joke to my colleagues that I was just going to be a resident therapist forever, and honestly, that I wasn't sure I would even want to be a therapist anymore by the time I got to the end of it. Many therapists find wonderful residency sites, where they feel supported with clients, encouraged to maintain a work-life balance, paid adequately, and all around joyful. I was not one of those therapists. For one reason or another, my residency sites included a tremendous amount of weekly tasks. I was often running 20+ hours of group therapy weekly alongside providing 15 or so individual therapy sessions, topped off with mountains of paperwork.

However, because of my clients, all of this felt worth it. I found that I have a natural skill as a therapist, and a desire to continue to learn how to be more effective. The feeling of seeing a client gain a healing insight, or take steps to change their life for the better made my heart overflow.

Yet I was tired and burned out. My main stressor as a resident was coming up with group material. In moments where I had the time, I definitely did not have the energy. The agencies I worked in usually offered up some sort of "curriculum." This meant a worksheet from 1975 (no offense to the year 1975!), or a 5-page group outline that was missing pages 2 and 4. Sometimes, depending on the funding of the agency, they had books available to therapists to research and create group content from. I had already ordered several wordy books looking for group therapy ideas. Wordy books are useful, but not super practical for the burned out, out-of-time-and-energy therapist.

I needed a workbook I could turn to that was already all laid out. One where I could look at it 20 minutes before a group was about to start. Something I could trust, and feel a genuine sense of readiness to roll with. I needed this workbook material to be evidence based, relevant, and geared towards my clients. I brought my passion as a therapist to every group, and just needed material that met me halfway. This didn't exist for me to buy, so I made one myself. I am now sharing that workbook with you.

I made *Ten Great Therapy Groups* based on my ten best groups ran throughout my extensive background as a group therapist. These are groups I developed using evidence-based materials and tweaked over ten years. They have been run over and over again with clients and have always yielded great feedback. Whether you are a resident, licensed therapist, or a groups facilitator, I know you are bringing your best to your groups and I have created a workbook I believe can work well with any personal style you may have. I have run these groups with the street homeless population and with the high-earning CEO population. They work for both because they can be adapted for both. The prompts in this workbook speak to the humanness in all of us. They facilitate bonding, empathy, and trust (the most healing aspects of group therapy, after all). They also offer up some pretty useful information.

As I mentioned before, I primarily worked in with substance abuse population. *Ten Great Therapy Groups* is written with that population in mind, and offers educational materials, activities, and group processing prompts. The groups can be run one at a time (for around 1.5-3 hours) or they can be broken up into several smaller groups. There are over 20 hours of group material at your disposal. Many of the groups can be adapted to a non-substance abuse population as they include broader topics within the realms of: emotional management, recovery from substance abuse and/or ill mental health, and building healthy relationships. My goal was that this adaptation does not take you more than 20 minutes to prepare.

I also hope that you learn from my group formatting, and can re-create more groups based on it. When you lean into something within your personal life that speaks to you on a healing level, I hope you can loosely follow this format to turn that into a group you can effectively and passionately deliver. Let *Ten Great Therapy Groups* both have your back and inspire you. Most of all, wherever you are in this journey of the healing professions, know that you are doing a great job and you deserve all of the support this world has to offer.

Instructions

Before I get into instructions to help you navigate this workbook and get the most out of *Ten Great Therapy Groups*, I want to remind you of the following truth:

The healing part about group therapy is the *group*. Take the pressure off yourself. You have a major role in the group's success, but the members will have to meet you halfway. They will only get out of the group what they put into the group. Group therapy by definition is different than individual therapy because it relies on the support of other people going through a similar experience. Group members practice healing when they feel heard, understood, empathized with, and not alone. Consider that all of these objectives can be met regardless if your topic "sucks" or you forget an important fact. Group therapy is relationship based and your job is simply to create the environment and allow the group relationships to work their magic.

The Workbook Set Up:

Each group is broken up into two columns. On the left-hand side, you will see the individual sections of the group along with any information for you as the facilitator.

On the right-hand side you will see the content for you to share with the group members.

The sections are broken up based on the activity such as "check-in," "group discussion," etc. They are meant to flow seamlessly into one another, and also offer points for you to start and stop the group depending on your time.

At the beginning of each group you will see the general outline of what the group is about and the materials you will need. I have also made a note of whether you will need to make any copies of worksheets before you start.

Worksheets are found in the last pages of each group along with any sources used in the material.

My vision is that you are able to use the group outlines for a good foundation for content, while bringing your own style and personality into the experience

Let's Get Started

Group One: Letting Go

Group topic summary:

This group topic is within the realm of mindfulness as it teaches clients the practice of letting go of thoughts, feelings, and experiences that no longer serve them. By the end of the group, the goal is that group members gain a new coping skill and thus have more tools for managing distress.

Materials: Clients will need some paper and a pen.

Length: About 1.5-2 hours (give or take, depending on the group)

Make copies of Handout 1.1 and 1.2 before starting the group.

Check in:

(10 minutes)

Pro Tip #1: Write the check-in prompts up on your board to help the clients remember what info to share.

Pro Tip #2: Write each client's first name and goal up on the board in a place you can return to it later.

Clients go around the room one at a time and check in with the following prompts:

1. How are you feeling today?

2. Did you have any cravings/urges last night (and if so, how did you overcome them)?

3. What is your goal today for group?

Introduction to Topic:

Today we are learning a new coping skill, the skill of "Letting Go" (no, this is nothing to do with *Frozen*) this is about learning to remain objective when distressing thoughts, feelings, and experiences are taking place in the present moment. When we remain objective, we can actively choose whether the distressing situation will impact us and how we preserve our sense of wellbeing no matter what life throws at us.

Group Discussion:

(5-10 minutes)

This first group discussion is a chance for group members to explore the meaning behind "Letting Go".

These questions prompt a small discussion about the concept of intention vs. failure. "Giving Up" is usually associated with a failure of some kind, while "Letting Go" is associated with the empowerment of intentionally releasing negativity.

Discussion Questions:

1. What is the difference between "Letting Go" and "Giving Up"?

2. How often are you holding onto various distressing situations out of fear of "Giving Up" on them?

3. Do you think it is possible to truly be able to Let Go?

Group Discussion:

(10 minutes)

Letting Go as a coping skill can be highly useful when applied to the right situation.

Some answers previous groups have given:

"When someone cuts you off in traffic."

"When you are thinking about something that already happened and cannot be changed."

"When you are feeling self-conscious about something."

"When you set boundaries and some one does not like it."

(Letting go is useful in such instances because it puts us in control of our mental health and lives. Letting Go is for when we deeply care about something, but we also need to protect ourselves and return to the present moment.)

Explore what situations Letting Go would be a useful coping skill for and discuss why.

Group Activity:

(10 minutes)

Group members can experiene the concept of Letting Go through the poem, and in the upcoming exercises they can experience it directly for themselves. Members may benefit from a copy of the poem depending on their ability to follow along by listening.

Read poem "She Let Go" by Reverend Safire Rose. found in Handout 1.1 to the group.

Discussion Questions:

What did you like about the poem?

What did you dislike about the poem?

BreakTime:

(10 minutes)

Independent Journaling Activity:

(15-20 minutes)

Some clients will use the time to think of as many answers as possible. Others may write "one word" answers. That's okay! Model Letting Go as the group practitioner and only request those who finish early remain quiet until you announce that time is up.

Consider playing soothing music while clients journal their answers.

During the group discussion, we will not ask clients to share memories unless you have a very safe, closed, group, as memories may be related to traumatic experiences

(Questions available as a handout in worksheet 1.2 at the end of this group chapter)

Journal Prompts:

1. Thoughts about myself I want to Let Go of are:

2. Thoughts about others that I want to Let Go of are:

3. Difficult emotions I am ready to Let Go of:

4. Memories that I feel ready to Let Go of:

5. Unfulfilled wishes and dreams I am ready to Let Go of are:

6. People I am ready to Let Go of are:

Group Discussion:

(10-15 minutes)

This group discussion is for clients to process their answers in the independent activity. As you introduce the discussion, consider making the safety disclaimer.

Discuss answers to journal questions

We want this group to feel safe for everybody. Only share information with the group that you feel ready to share. It is okay if you do not feel ready to share any of your answers with the group, but remain supportive to your fellow group members as they practice vulnerability in this setting.

Responses to keep in mind that will foster the group process:

1. Can anyone relate?

2. How can we (the group) support you?

Group Discussion Questions:

1. How did the exercise go for everyone?

2. What thoughts did you feel ready to let go of?

3. What emotions did you feel ready to let go of?

4. How did it go answering the unfulfilled dreams and wishes question?

5. What did you find that could make it difficult to let go?

6. Any thoughts about this process?

Group Activity:

(10 minutes)

When clients actively Let Go of the situations that they listed in the first activity, they will need guidance on what to replace the space with.

Consider the following if clients are having difficulty thinking of healthy replacements:

Thought of self: I am good enough, I don't need to be perfect, I am doing my best, I deserve this, I am worthy of love

Thoughts of Others: Most people are focused on themselves, they are doing their best, people are entitled to their opinion

Emotions: Gratitude, peace, love, freedom

Memories: Happy memories from childhood, memories of success, comforting memories of my favorite season.

When we Let Go, we need to replace what we let go of!

For the things you decided to let go of, let's think together of healthy replacements.

Prompts:

1. When I Let Go of certain thoughts about myself, I will replace them with:

2. When I let go of what I think of others I will replace my thoughts with:

3. When I Let Go of certain emotions, I will replace them with:

4. When I let go of difficult memories, I will replace them with these memories:

Group Meditation:

(10 minutes)

See handout 1.3 for guided meditation script.

Read meditation out loud, slowly and calmly.

.

I am going to take you through a guided Letting Go meditation. You can choose whether to close your eyes or keep your gaze open softly. Meditation is part of the tool kit for Letting Go.

Final Processing Question:

What was the meditation experience like for you?

w2w

This group was an introduction to the process of Letting Go as a coping skill. In this group we:

1. Gained a more in-depth understanding of Letting Go and where it can be useful.

2. Explored where we can practice Letting Go in our own lives.

3. Identified healthy replacements we can Draw In after we Let Go.

4. Practiced physically letting go through mindfulness and mediation.

Check Out Questions:

1. What is one thing you learned today?

2. How will you implement what you learned?

3. Did you meet your goal set out at the beginning of group?

4. What could have been better about group today?

She Let Go

She let go.

Without a thought or a word, she let go.

She let go of fear. She let go of the judgments.

She let go of the confluence of opinions swarming around her head.

She let go of the committee of indecision within her.

She let go of all the 'right' reasons. Wholly and completely,

without hesitation or worry, she just let go.

She didn't ask anyone for advice. She didn't read a

book on how to let go… She didn't search the scriptures.

She just let go.

She let go of all of the memories that held her back.

She let go of all of the anxiety that kept her from moving forward.

She let go of the planning and all of the calculations about how to do it just right.

She didn't promise to let go.

She didn't journal about it.

She didn't write the projected date in her day-timer.

She made no public announcement and put no ad in the paper.

(Cont. on next page)

She didn't check the weather report or read her daily horoscope.

She just let go.

She didn't analyze whether she should let go.

She didn't call her friends to discuss the matter.

She didn't do a five-step Spiritual Mind Treatment.

She didn't call the prayer line.

She didn't utter one word.

She just let go.

No one was around when it happened.

There was no applause or congratulations.

No one thanked her or praised her.

No one noticed a thing.

Like a leaf falling from a tree, she just let go.

There was no effort. There was no struggle.

It wasn't good and it wasn't bad.

It was what it was, and it is just that.

In the space of letting go, she let it all be.

A small smile came over her face.

A light breeze blew through her.

And the sun and the moon shone forevermore.

-Reverend Safire Rose

Independent Journal Prompts

Thoughts about myself I want to Let Go of are:

Thoughts about others that I want to Let Go of are:

Difficult emotions I am ready to Let Go of:

Memories that I feel ready to Let Go of:

Unfulfilled wishes and dreams I am ready to Let Go of are:

People I am ready to Let Go of are:

Things that could make it difficult to Let Go:

Letting Go will be an especially useful coping skill for me during:

Figure 1.3

Guided Meditation on Letting Go

Let's begin by getting into a comfortable seated position. Close your eyes or keep them open and soften your gaze. Bring your attention to your breath. Notice how your stomach expands with the inbreath and relaxes with the out breath.

We will start by slowing your breathing down to a count of 5. Inhale: 1-2-3-4-5, Hold: 1-2, Exhale: 1-2-3-4-5. We will do that two more times:

Inhale: 1-2-3-4-5, Hold: 1-2, Exhale: 1-2-3-4-5.

Inhale: 1-2-3-4-5, Hold: 1-2, Exhale: 1-2-3-4-5.

Now bring your attention to the top of your head. Start scanning your attention down your face, relaxing each muscle as you go. Relax your forehead, relax your eyes, relax your cheeks, relax your mouth.

Follow the relaxation downward. Relax your shoulders, relax your left arm, your left hand. Relax your right arm, your right hand.

Relax your chest, your belly, your hips. Relax your left thigh, your left shin, your left foot. Relax your right thigh, your right shin, your right foot.

In this state of total relaxation, take your mind to the thoughts about yourself you felt ready to Let Go of. Hear them repeating to you in your mind (silently count 1-2-3-4-5)

Now, imagine a big swirling circle drawing all of the thoughts in. Give the circle a color. Imagine the pressure of it growing in your forehead. Take a big inhale.

Exhale the swirling circle out of your forehead. Pass the thoughts up into the sky. Relax your forehead. Feel the free space you created. Peacefulness. Calm. Relaxed.

Turn your attention to the Emotions you felt ready to Let Go of. Feel them repeating in your heart (silently count 1-2-3-4-5)

Imagine a big swirling circle drawing all of the emotions in. Give the circle a color. Feel the pressure of them growing in your heart. Take a big inhale.

Exhale the swirling circle out of your heart. Pass the emotions up into the sky. Relax your shoulders, calm your breathing, listen to your heart beating freely.

Finally, turn your attention to the memories you felt ready to go of. See them replaying in your minds eye. (silently count 1-2-3-4-5)

Figure 1.3 cont.

Imagine a big swirling circle drawing all of the memories in. Give the circle a color. Feel the pressure of them growing in your belly. Take a big inhale.

Exhale the swirling circle out of your belly. Pass the memories up into the sky. Relax your breathing, calm your belly.

Now Imagine a beautiful light cascading down all around you. Down past your head, your chest, circling you entirely. In this light, are all of the wonderful thoughts, emotions, and memories you wanted to Draw In.

Feel the pleasant thoughts trickle down into your mind and settle into the free space. What thoughts are now there? (silently count 1-2-3-4-5)

Next feel the pleasant emotions trickle down into your heart and settle into the free space. What emotions are now there? (silently count 1-2-3-4-5)

Feel the pleasant memories trickle down into your belly and settle into the free space. What memories are now there? (silently count 1-2-3-4-5)

Take a big inhale. Exhale. Feel the lightness in your body as you let go of negativity and draw in positivity.

Another big inhale.

Exhale.

Know that what you drew in is with you for the rest of the day, feel the joy and gratitude from this freedom.

Feel your body start to wake up with excitement. Wiggle your toes. Wiggle your fingers. Scrunch your shoulders up. Release Them.

Open your eyes.

Welcome back.

Group Two: Spirituality

Group Topic Summary:

This group topic is prompted to explore the spiritual side of healing. The intention of this group is for clients to build a deeper connection with one another as well as begin thinking about the role of spirituality within their life and healing process. By the end of the group, group members will develop insight into their spirituality and explore the use of spirituality for connection to one another and as a tool for supporting the healing process.

Materials: Clients will need some paper and a pen.

If you decide to use the bonus activity you will need: magazines, glue, scissors, markers, and construction paper.

Length: About 1-2 hours (give or take, depending on the group)

Make copies of Handout 2.1 before starting the group.

Check in:

(10 minutes)

Pro Tip #1: Write the check-in prompts up on your board to help the clients remember what info to share.

Pro Tip #2: Write each client's first name and goal up on the board in a place you can return to it later.

Clients go around the room one at a time and check in with the following prompts:

1. How are you feeling today?

2. Did you have any cravings/urges last night (and if so, how did you overcome them)?

3. What is your goal today for group?

Introduction to Topic:

Today we are diving deeper into spirituality. This topic is not about individual religions and we'll have some group rules as we discuss this topic:

1. We will respect the different spiritual views expressed during this group.

2. We will be non-judgmental for one another.

As we further explore spirituality today, you can get the sense of whether spirituality can be a tool for your healing process.

Group Discussion:

(20-25 minutes)

Go through each phrase individually and discuss as a group the various personal experiences that support whether the statement "helps or hurts." Allow clients to share as much or a little as they feel comfortable with.

Do the following common statements *help* or *hurt* your healing process?

1. God will not give you more than you can handle.

2. When one door closes, the universe opens another.

3. Everything happens for a reason.

4. Your thoughts manifest your reality.

5. Karma helps people get what they deserve.

6. The universe has shaken you to awaken you.

7. Gratitude is the best attitude.

Group Brainstorm:

(10-15 minutes)

We want to ground the group in spirituality as this can apply across any religious background and can be adapted to the individual. This conversation is empowering for clients to personalize what their spirituality means to them.

Some differences to consider:

Religion: cultural, particular, rules, ethics, obligations, set of certain beliefs based on texts

Spirituality: Universal, personal sense of meaning, relationship based, no formal organization, self-discovery

Walking in nature, meditating, rituals, holidays, journaling, listening to music, drawing, singing, yoga

Spiritual Expression can help us stay strong, process emotions, deal with cravings, lift our mood, and give us a sense of meaning.

As a group discuss the difference between sprituality and religion in a group brainstorm:

Religion:

Spirituality:

(Write answers on board)

Discussion Questions:

What can be some forms of spiritual expression?

How can spirituality be useful in recovering from drug and alcohol use and/or mental health issues?

Group Activity:

(25-30 minutes)

If you have enough space and materials, you can also have clients go up to the board and write their own word(s)

Word examples:

Faith, awe, healing, light, peace, hope, acceptance, gratitude, peace, connection, forgiveness, etc.

Sentence Examples:

I have faith in my recovery

I am in awe of my strength

(Depending how many clients are in the group, you can have people go around twice with sentences to contribute)

Read the finished poem/product out loud.

Flow into the group discussion below:

What words come to mind that are associated with spirituality? Shout them out and I'll write them up on the board.

Now that we have this list of words, everyone take a few minutes to write down some sentences out of the words on the board. Your sentences should relate the words to healing from addiction and/or mental health issues.

Don't think too hard, whatever comes to mind is good enough!

Now that everyone has some sentences ready, choose your best one and write it on our board. We will go in order around the group. It's okay if it doesn't "make sense," just go with the flow.

Who wants to read what we made out loud?

Group Discussion:

(5-10 minutes)

This is a time to process and celebrate the poem or story that was created.

Groups may want to draw images to go alongside the poem, create it into a rap or a song lyric, take photos of it.

Question Prompts:

1. Does the poem bring about any feelings/thoughts/reactions?

2. Does this poem demonstrate spirituality?

3. Does this poem bring any images to mind?

Bonus Activity:

(20-30 minutes)

Create a collage based on the group poem. Let your imagination roll!

Break Time:

(10 minutes)

Independent Activity:

(15 minutes)

This is a worksheet to prompt clients to explore inward the spiritual practices they believe will support their healing.

(In the event that a client feels completely against spirituality- prompt them to fill out the worksheet using the word "connect" instead of "spiritual" or "reaching out" to focus on improving relationships overall.)

Hand out the worksheet (Handout 2.1) for clients to fill out independently.

Group Discussion:

(10 minutes)

This group discussion is for clients to process their answers in the independent activity, as well as share their ideas with other group members in the event that they struggled to think of practices themselves.

Discussion Questions:

1. How did the exercise go for everyone?

2. What sort of practices did you identify?

3. How could a morning spiritual practice help you?

4. How could an evening spiritual practice hep you?

Closing Statements and Check Out:

(10-15 minutes)

One by one, go around the group and have clients answer the check-out questions.

Pro Tip #3: Write the check out questions on the board to help the client's remember what is asked.

Question #4 can be uncomfortable. However, it is an opportunity for you to model how to recieve constructive criticism in a positive manner. The answers to this question will also give you feedback on what to alter in this group to best fit your population.

This group was an introduction to Spirituality within our healing process. In this group we:

1. Gained a more in-depth understanding of Spirituality.

2. Discussed how it helps or hurts us.

3. Practiced using spirituality to connect as a group for a group poem.

4. Identified ways to implement spirituality within our own lives.

Check Out Questions:

1. What is one thing you learned today?

2. How will you implement what you learned?

3. Did you meet your goal set out at the beginning of group?

4. What could have been better about group today?

Spirituality Worksheet

Spirituality as a healing tool requires cultivating your relationship with yourself (inward), others (outward), and the world above you (upward). Think of ways you can connect to each part and write them in and around the diamond. Also record spiritual practices that you can do each morning and evening to support your healing.

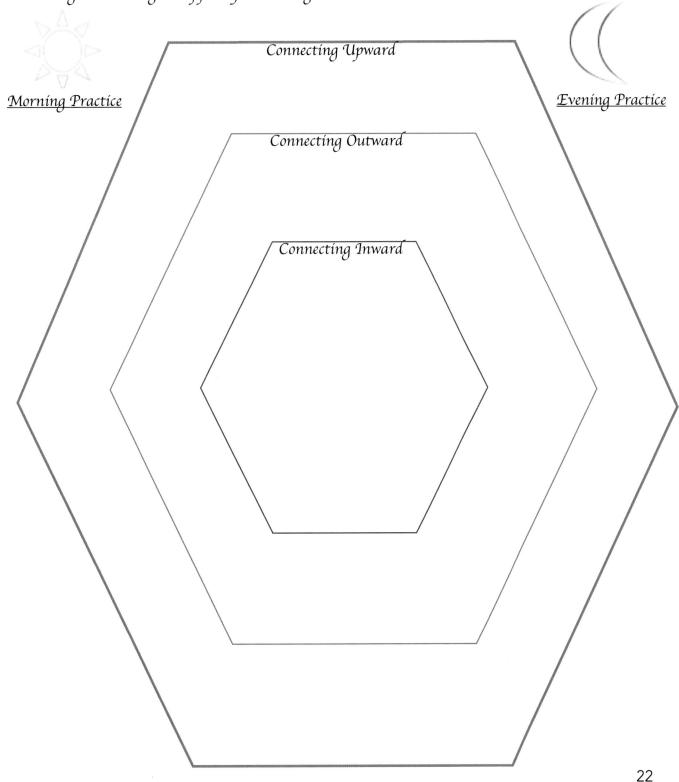

Connecting Upward

Connecting Outward

Connecting Inward

<u>Morning Practice</u>

<u>Evening Practice</u>

Group Three: Self Esteem

Group topic summary:

Our self-esteem impacts several areas of our life. The intention of this group is to explore the origins of our self-esteem, and how we can work to change/improve our self-esteem. Group members are empowered to apply self-compassion and begin the healing process of improving their inner self-dialogue. By the end of the group, the goal is that group members gain tools to raise their self-esteem and change their perceptions of themselves and others.

Materials: Clients will need some paper and a pen.

Length: About 1.5-2 hours (give or take, depending on the group)

Make copies of Handout 3.1 and 3.2 before starting the group.

Check in:

(10 minutes)

Pro Tip #1: Write the check-in prompts up on your board to help the clients remember what info to share.

Pro Tip #2: Write each client's first name and goal up on the board in a place you can return to it later.

Clients go around the room one at a time and check in with the following prompts:

1. How are you feeling today?

2. Did you have any cravings/urges last night (and if so, how did you overcome them)?

3. What is your goal today for group?

Introduction to Topic:

Today we are talking all about self-esteem. Our self-esteem can impact several areas of our life. Self-esteem is all about our working perception of who we are in this world. We are going to explore where self-esteem comes from and how to cultivate a healthy self-esteem. Cultivating a healthy self-esteem is a huge tool for us to use in our healing journey.

Group Brainstorm:

(25-30 minutes)

Some examples of what clients usually report:

Ages 0-5:

Parents, siblings, toys, extended family

Ages 5-12

Kids at school, cartoons, sports or hobbies, classroom behaviors, if you get in "trouble," bullying, parents, siblings, home-life.

Ages 13-18

Your friends at school, grades, extra-curricular activities, your body, if you have

Write the following categories on the board (leaving space below for the brainstorm):

<u>Ages</u>

1.   0-5
2.   5-12
3.   13-18
4.   18-25
5.   35+

Together, lets identify the people and factors that impact or decide a person's self-esteem during the various age groups, pulling from your own life experience. We will go age group by age group and I'll write down the answers you shout out.

(After a list is created) Let's together, as a group, analyze the results:

a car, parents/caretakers, if you are in a romantic relationship, TV, social media (major factor now-a-days!), how much money your family has, drugs, alcohol, clothes, texting, sex, mental heath

Ages 18-25

Going to college or not, amount of money you have, if you're in a relationship or not, drug use, health, where you live (at home or moving out), mental health

Ages 35+

Where you live, what job you have, if you're married, have kids or don't have kids, physical health, mental health, drug & alcohol use

Here we are promoting insight into the cumulative effect of negative self-esteem experiences. They can often happen when we are young, too young to remember, and then continue onward in a pattern through-out our lives.

Being responsible for our own self-esteem can be uplifting and empowering for some clients. Other clients may demonstrate nervousness about the responsibility this implies if they accept it to be true. We want to show empathy for that experience and normalize the feelings of uncertainty that come alongside making changes.

Analyzing Questions:

1.   Does anyone have anything they want to share about their experience of making and seeing this list?

2.   What do you notice about the list?

A major take-away is that up until age 18- a large part of our self-esteem is dependent on factors that are out of our control- we are for the most part forced to go to school and stay with our caretakers. This sets the stage for feeling like our self-esteem "Happens to Us"- and that once it has happened, we are destined to just live out whatever we experienced when we were younger.

Let's say when you were young, ages 0-5, your parents or caretakers weren't very skilled at telling you "good-job!". Maybe they didn't understand you were a kid, and they expected you to behave and function like an adult. That could definitely negatively impact your self-esteem. What would happen to you in your next stage if you started with a lower self-esteem in the previous stage?

The factors that contribute to self-esteem also tend to shrink in adulthood. Many of the factors are now within our control. That means that we can raise our self-esteems ourselves- through the choices we make and our inner dialogue. ***Our self-esteem is now our responsibility.***

Discussion Question:

What is it like to consider that you are more in charge of your self-esteem than you realized? Is anyone surprised by that? Is that something you agree with or disagree with?

Break Time:

(10 minutes)

Group Discussion:

(15-20 minutes)

Before the break, we looked at some of the factors influencing self-esteem in our lifetime. Now I am going to share with you a story that starts to speak to the ways in which we take our experiences with us and perhaps negatively impact our self-esteems ourselves.

Read the story in Handout 3.1

Prompting Questions:

1. What did this story mean to you?

2. How does this story relate to our self-esteem?

3. What does this story suggest we can do to "break our ropes"?

Independent Activity:

(15-20 minutes)

Give clients time to write out 3 or more "ropes." Examples of "ropes"

Pass out worksheet (Handout) 3.2

This is a simple worksheet where you are asked to identify 3 "ropes" (negative things you were told about yourself or experienced) that you believe you might still

"I won't go to college because people in my life don't do further education."

"I'm not good at leading people."

Rope cutting statement example:

I am a compassionate and caring leader.

be chained to today.

Once you have some ropes identified: Ask yourself: "What else could be true?" to support your ability to identify rope-breaking statements or experiences that will cut the ropes tying you down.

Be as detailed and fearless in this inventory as you feel safe to be. Sometimes it can be difficult to think from the ground-up about our ropes. Another way to identify ropes is to think in the present moment: where are you having difficulties? Then, if we work our way backwards from that, we usually find an old rope tying us down.

Group Discussion:

(15-20 minutes)

At first glance, therapists will often assume all ropes may just be "self-limiting beliefs" and that they may not be "true."

Be careful in this assumption, as sometimes the ropes can be from traumatic experiences, memories, or strong emotional experiences. Therefore, they could have very well been true at one point in the client's life. Help the client choose a new perspective for the future while honoring the truth of the past.

The ropes can show up in words, pictures, sounds, and/or memories.

Discussion Questions:

1. How was this activity for you?

2. Share with us some of the ropes you identified.

3. What helps you break the ropes?

4. Do you feel that the ropes stay broken once they are cut? If not, how can we maintain the "break" and make sure the rope does not grow back together?

Group Activity:

(20-30 minutes)

#1: This question will help you get a feel for where the group is currently and allow you to meet them where they are.

#2: Many of us are taught that we have to be "perfect" in order to be allowed to have a good self-esteem. This is especially meaningful to challenge within the group space.

The key elements to raising our self-esteem are not rooted in our past. They are instead rooted in the "here and now." We can take steps within these categories TODAY.

Some examples for each category:

(Values): end friendships with toxic people, show up for my kid's events, eat healthy and take care of my body.

(Small Goals): eat a healthy breakfast today, be on-time to group, start saving money.

(Self-Compassion): I forgive myself for pushing away my friend trying to help me- I understand I was doing the best I could at the time, I am allowed to make mistakes and learn from them, I can apologize for my behavior and forgive myself even if the other person cannot.

We have looked at the origins/past and how old patterns get brought into our lives. The last exercise of the group is to come up with ways to raise our self-esteems in the present.

Discussion Questions:

1. So how do we actually raise our self-esteem?

PUBLIC SERVICE ANNOUNCMENT: WE DO NOT RAISE OUR SELF-ESTEEMS BY BECOMING PERFECT!!!

2. Does perfection exist?

There are several ways to raise our self-esteems. Let's look at some ways to get started. On the board write the following categories:

Aligning with our Values

Setting small goals and Completing them

Practicing Self-Compassion

As a group, what are some examples within each category ? (Bulk of the time is spent on brainstorming and writing these up on the board)

It can feel a little silly at first, but just like when we are raising the self-esteems of our children, we celebrate success. We must apply the same joy to ourselves and develop an inner dialogue of saying "good job" when we complete a goal. When we make mistakes, we practice self-compassion to what happened- even if our mistake is misaligned with our values.

Closing Statements and Check Out:

(10-15 minutes)

One by one, go around the group and have clients answer the check-out questions.

Pro Tip #3: Write the check-out questions on the board to help the clients remember what is asked.

This group was all about Self-Esteem: how it develops and how we can improve it. In this group we:

1. Explored the origins of Self-Esteem

2. Used story to gain a deeper understanding of the development of self-esteem.

3. Identified old patterns and beliefs and re-framed them to support overcoming our own limits.

4. Planned for integrating improvement of self-esteem into our lives.

Check Out Questions:

1. What is one thing you learned today?

2. How will you implement what you learned?

3. Did you meet your goal set out at the beginning of group?

4. What could have been better about group today?

How Baby Elephants are Trained

Elephants in captivity are trained, at an early age, not to roam. One leg of a baby elephant is tied with a rope to a wooden post planted in the ground.

The rope confines the baby elephant to an area, determined by the length of the rope. Initially the baby elephant tries to break free from the rope, but the rope is too strong.

The baby elephant "learns" that it can't break the rope.

When the elephant grows up and is strong, it could easily break the same rope. But because it "learned" that it couldn't break the rope when it was young, the adult elephant believes that it still can't break the rope, so it doesn't even try!

Humans operate in a similar way. We learned something about ourselves at an early age and still believe it as an adult. Even though it may not be true, we operate as if it was.

Fortunately, humans are born with the ability to make conscious choices- an important step in changing how you perceive it yourself.

-

Author Unknown.

My Ropes	My Rope Cutting Statements

Group Four: Coping Skills

Group Topic Summary:

The goal of this group is that group members will be able to identify where they are using maladaptive coping mechanisms and be able to replace them with healthy coping skills. Clients will be encouraged to understand what coping skills are and how to apply them in various situations. Clients will develop awareness of healthy coping skills and increase their understanding what coping skills are and when to apply them.

Materials: Clients will need some paper and pens, scissors, tape and coloring materials like markers or crayons.

Length: About 1.5-2 hours (give or take, depending on the group)

Make copies of Handout 4.1 before group.

Check in:

(10 minutes)

Pro Tip #1: Write the check-in prompts up on your board to help the clients remember what info to share.

Pro Tip #2: Write each client's first name and goal up on the board in a place you can return to it later.

Clients go around the room one at a time and check in with the following prompts:

1. How are you feeling today?

2. Did you have any cravings/urges last night (and if so, how did you overcome them)?

3. What is your goal today for group?

Introduction to Topic:

Today we are going to talk all about coping skills. You may have heard of coping skills before, and are probably already using several to get through each day. The goal of this group is to deepen your understanding of coping skills and to encourage you to develop and apply coping skills that are proven to work in your daily life.

Group Discussion:

(10 minutes)

Coping skills are a set of tools or activities that we do on purpose with the goal of reducing whatever stress or tension we are experiencing.

The purpose of this brief discussion is to warm the group members up about the topic, and for you to gauge the group members' current understanding of coping skills.

Warm Up Questions:

1. What are some examples of coping skills?

2. Where did you learn coping skills? (From your family? T.V.? Growing up?)

3. How do we know if a coping skill works?

4. Be Honest--- do you always use your coping skills? If not- why?

Question #4 normalizes the reality that despite knowing about coping skills, we don't always use them. This can be for various reasons that will be unique to each individual.

Group Brainstorm & Education:

(10-20 minutes)

Unhealthy coping skills examples: using drugs, drinking alcohol, arguing, fighting, cussing, taking revenge, self-harming, over-eating, driving.

Examples of what prior groups have said:

"because it makes whatever stress is occurring instantly go away (doesn't resolve it). Or we want other people to suffer the same way that we are."

Question Prompts:

1. Before we get into healthy coping skills- what are some examples of unhealthy coping skills?

2. If we know a coping skill is unhealthy- why do we still do it?

3. When did you develop most of the automatic coping skills you use today?

Another factor to consider, is that most of the time we are using coping skills we developed a LONG time ago- maybe when we were kids, or adolescents, and expecting them to work now as adults. Something that worked when we were a teen- for example: yelling and screaming or skipping school, probably doesn't work as adults because it could result in some serious consequences like losing our jobs or hurting our relationships.

It is our responsibility to recognize when we are using an old coping skill and to actively work on replacing it with a newer, healthy coping skill.

Another reason might be that we simply never learned the coping skill that actually works in the moment. For example, if we saw our parents handle rejection by drinking or fighting, we might have no idea what to do with rejection simply because we've never seen it "handled" well.

Not every coping skill works for the same event. For example, if my main coping skill is to journal, that might work really well

1. Calming:

Take a warm bath, light a candle, drink a warm cup of tea, reading a book, taking a nap, do slow yoga, listen to slow music, draw, color in a color-book, look out of the window, meditate, take a mindfulness walk. Speak nicely to yourself, forgive yourself, normalize your feelings, give yourself space to feel emotions, accept yourself for who you are.

2. Distracting:

Watch favorite T.V. show, scroll through social media, bake or cook something, clean up the area around you, talk to a friend on the phone, do a puzzle, read a book, make a collage, listen to music, follow a guided meditation of going to the beach, plan your weekend activities. Think about your to-do list, focus on remembering positive memories, set a safe-time to return to thoughts about the present distressing event, count to 100, do math problems in your mind.

3. Processing/understanding:

Journal- free write on the topic, talk to therapist, text or calling a good friend, make a pros/cons list, draw images that clarify the situation, create categories of "thoughts, feelings, and behaviors" and bullet journal responses for each, set a timer for 10-minutes just to think, allow yourself to "sleep on it". Slow down any racing thoughts, practice positive affirmations, focus on your strengths.

4. Physical:

Go for a run, go to the gym, do yoga, go for a walk, scream into a pillow, punch a pillow, jumping jacks, dance, volunteer, walk away from stressor, play with your pet, take a boxing class, take a cold shower, squeeze your muscles and relax them one by one. Practice

for situations I am trying to process and better understand. However, if I'm feeling really angry about a situation, I might need something more physical to properly reduce the stress and tension before I can sit down and journal. Journaling is probably not the best coping skill to use "in the moment."

The categories I am about to write on the board each refer to the different outcomes we need depending on the triggering event. Let's brain storm about some of the healthy coping skills that fit into each category:

On the board write the following categories with some space underneath for brainstorming together as a group:

1. Calming

2. Distracting

3. Processing/Understanding

4. Physical Change

(Brainstorm together as a group which coping skills fit in each category- both external coping skills such as activities and internal coping skills such as thoughts and self-talk).

7-11 breathing (breathe in for 7 seconds and breathe out for 11 seconds). Repeat to yourself "all is well and I am relaxing."

Keep items up on the board during the break

Break Time:

(10 minutes)

Independent Activity:

(25-30 minutes)

See Handout 4.1 for box cut-out

I am going to pass out small strips of paper. On the paper, write down situations that are CURRENTLY causing you stress and/or tension. If there is nothing currently happening, think back to your most recent stressful event. Write them down on the paper and then cut them out and fold them up into smaller pieces and set aside.

Next, I am passing out a handout that we will cut out and turn into a box. Use your scissors to cut on the bold lines and fold on the dotted lines. Use tape to assemble your box- but don't close it yet!

Color and decorate the box in a way that honors you, and write on the outside of the box the coping skills you think could work to help manage the situations you wrote on the paper.

Once you are finished, put your folded strips of paper in the center of the box before you totally close it with tape.

You might need to make a few different boxes depending on the situations you identified and the coping skills you would apply to manage them.

Group Discussion:

(25-30 minutes)

Prompt group members to share their experience and allow for any discussion points that may come up naturally.

Your box is a physical representation of coping skills in action. Coping skills don't necessarily "solve" the stressor, but they help us put the stressor "away" and return to our baseline level of functioning so that we can continue to enjoy our life and move forward. Your box is a tangible representation of your stressful event & experience contained safely by coping skills.

Some Discussion Prompts to Consider:

1. What do you notice about the box you created?

2. How do you feel about your stressful event now that it's in the box?

3. Did anyone write down coping skills to try that they haven't used before?

4. How was this exercise for you overall?

Final Group Activity:

(25-30 minutes)

Before we finish up today- there is one last exercise we are going to do together to practice using healthy coping skills. You will actually be able to use your phones for this! We are going to use this last part of group to focus on how powerful music can be as a coping skill, partly because there is music for every type of emotion!

I am going to assign stressful "emotions" or "situations" to each of you, your job is to write down songs that would be a healthy "coping" song to help you manage the stressful situation.

You can use your phone to google song lyrics, if you're going to listen to any songs please put the volume down low where only you can hear it putting your phone up to your ear.

Let's go around the group and everyone will get a chance to explain the situation to the group and play ONE of the songs you chose to help cope out loud. Remember to share with us why you chose the particular song.

(Depending on time you can allow them to play the whole song, but usually 30 seconds to a minute of the song is sufficient.)

Situations are at end of chapter in Handout 4.2

Assign the situations and give group members about 10 minutes to come up with songs they thing would help them "cope" with the situation.

This is meant to be a fun activity. Music is a powerful connector for all of us and sharing music with each other will help build group cohesion and will end the group on a positive note.

Closing Statements and Check Out:

(10-15 minutes)

One by one, go around the group and have clients answer the check-out questions.

Pro Tip #3: Write the check-out questions on the board to help the clients remember what is asked.

This group was all about building and using healthy Coping Skills. In todays group, we:

1. Explored the unhealthy and healthy coping skills.

2. Practiced applying coping skills to a stressful life event.

3. Practiced applying music to cope with various stressful situations.

Check Out Questions:

1. What is one thing you learned today?

2. How will you implement what you learned?

3. Did you meet your goal set out at the beginning of group?

4. What could have been better about group today?

Square Box Template

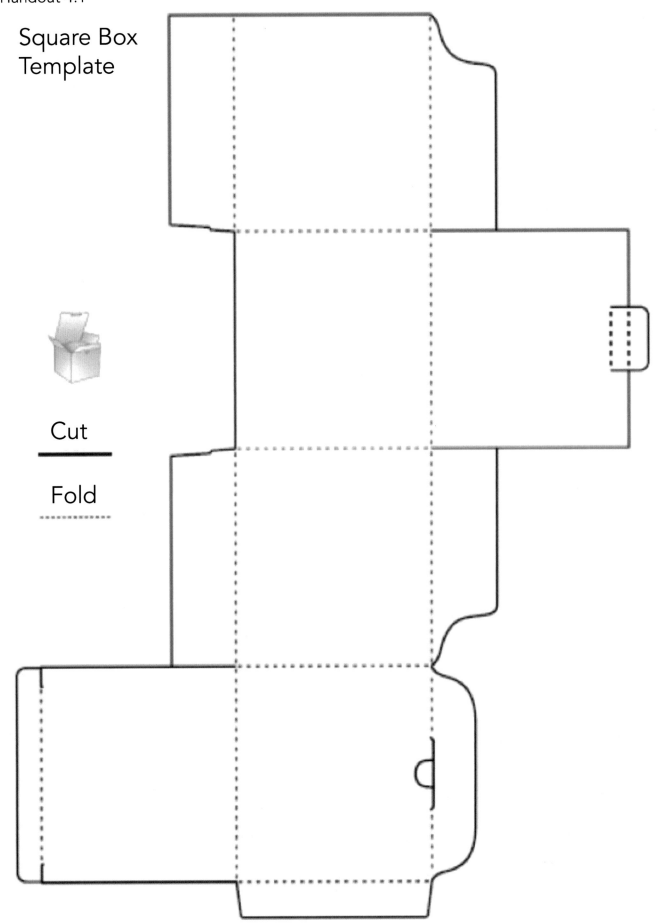

Cut
_____

Fold
- - - - - - -

Situations to Assign:

Your partner is giving you the silent treatment. This is hurting your feelings.	Lately you have between remembering a sad and difficult memory from childhood.
Someone rear-ends your car and then drives away.	You are worried about the "unknowns" in the future.
You're feeling anxiety about an upcoming presentation.	You are so bored with your job and struggling to stay awake.
Your depression is telling you that you're not doing "good enough."	You got blamed for something that you didn't do.
You're feeling lost about what direction to take your life in.	Someone you love tells you that they are disappointed in you.
Your friends got together without you and as a result you feel left out and lonely.	You're missing your ex- partner from your last relationship.
Everyone is doing great things on social media, and it feels like you're being left out.	You're experiencing guilt over a mistake you made years ago.
You were the target of a well-organized scam and lost $500.	You're in a lot of physical pain.

Group Five: Managing Triggers

Group topic summary:

"Triggers" refers to the various sights, sounds, and sensations that literally trigger the brain to start a chain reaction that, if not interrupted, can lead to relapse. By the end of the group, the goal is that group members will be able to identify their unique triggers as well as gain the tools and resources necessary to interrupt triggers and avoid relapse.

Materials: Clients will need some paper and pens.

Length: About 1.5-2 hours (give or take, depending on the group)

Make copies of Handouts 5.1 and 5.2 before starting the group.

Check in:

(10 minutes)

Pro Tip #1: Write the check-in prompts up on your board to help the clients remember what info to share.

Pro Tip #2: Write each client's first name and goal up on the board in a place you can return to it later.

Clients go around the room one at a time and check in with the following prompts:

1. How are you feeling today?

2. Did you have any cravings/urges last night (and if so, how did you overcome them)?

3. What is your goal today for group?

Introduction to Topic:

Today we are going to dive into learning more about triggers. You may have heard the word "trigger" so much lately that you are feeling pretty "over it." However, triggers are important to revisit over and over again as they are frequently referred to as the start of the relapse process. Today, we are going to explore your tools and resources you can use to manage triggers.

Group Discussion:

(20 minutes)

Group members may have various responses to this question depending on their exposure to the world of recovery.

Answer: Triggers are people, places, things, emotions, sensations (like sounds/smells) that remind the brain of the "feel good" chemicals it gets when a person uses drugs or alcohol. Triggers are considered the start of the chain reaction to relapse, and can go unnoticed or be noticed.

Triggers can be *external* in the environment around us, or *internal* such as feeling insecure, embarrassed, etc.

Prompting Questions:

1. So… what ARE triggers?

2. Can someone share their experience of being triggered?

3. What usually happens if you get triggered? (This answer will be different across group members)

(examples: feel anxious, want to use, feel trapped)

4. Has anyone ever had a trigger completely surprise them?

5. What do you do if you are triggered?

Examples: Alcohol commercials, smell of a BBQ, friends used to use with, text from dealer, the weather, the drive past the liquor store, anger, feeling tired/low energy, painful memory, etc.

Brief Education Session:

(10 minutes)

Once the brain is having a craving, it becomes increasingly difficult and unlikely to successfully avoid relapse. This is due to the physical and emotional intensity of a craving. Most of recovery focus is on how to manage cravings- especially in early recovery when it feels like they are happening non-stop without a break.

Sometimes it feels like we go from trigger to craving lightening fast, but we can interrupt the trigger from becoming a full-blown craving by gaining insight into this process and creating space to manage our thoughts.

Many of the strategies for managing triggers are similar to the strategies for managing cravings.

This is one of the most successful ways to avoid the cycle entirely.

On the board write the following:

Trigger ⟶ Craving ⟶ Relapse

Looking at this flow, what is it like to try to avoid relapse once you have a full-blown craving?

(hint: it's really hard!)

What about interrupting the process between trigger and craving? What is that like?

How can we interrupt a trigger?

Examples: Awareness that it happened, call a friend, focus on our "why", remove ourselves from the environment, go to a meeting, journal.

And finally, what about stopping this process from even starting? We can learn to avoid triggers all-together- But how can we do that?

We need to have insight into what our triggers are, where they are, and make plans to avoid them. In a situation where a trigger is un-avoidable, then we need to seriously plan around that trigger.

Group Activity:

(25-30 minutes)

Give group members about 20 minutes to discuss these events and create their management plan.

Example:

Triggers at a funeral: sadness, after-party open bar, existential thoughts (what's the point anyway?), peer pressure, social awkwardness, toasts

Plan: go with a sober-friend, don't attend after-party, journal to acknowledge your own emotions beforehand

(Break group members up into small groups.)

Assign the small groups the following prompts:

1. A Funeral

2. The Airport

3. A Cook-out

4. A Wedding

5. Happy Hour

Pass out handout 5.1

Explain the following to the group:

I have handed each group an event. Your instructions are to brainstorm together all of the triggers that could be in your event. Once you have identified as many triggers as you can, list some ways you could manage the trigger.

Remember to consider: people, places, things, emotions, and sensations

Break Time:

(10 minutes)

Group Discussion:

(15-20 minutes)

Prompt group members to share their findings and allow for any discussion points that may come up naturally.

Ask each group to present their event and the findings to the group around them.

Some discussion prompts to consider if you need them:

1. How was this activity for your group?

2. Has anyone ever been in this situation?

Remember to give positive reinforcement for group members for their hard work on this!

Supportively discuss this as a group:

Don't go to the event: This must be mentioned as it seems like a last resort, but sometimes it is the most logical answer. We usually have to make sacrifices for our goals, this can include not having the instant gratification of going to events. This might mean we let people down, or get a serious case of "FOMO" (fear of missing out), but recovery requires that we put ourselves and our wellbeing first, above all else.

This concept needs to be prompted in the group discussion following the activity if it does not come up naturally, as it promotes group cohesion and the feeling of support among the group that others are "missing out" on things as well in order to build a meaningful and healthy future.

3. Any other ideas for how to manage the triggers?

What about not going to the event at all?

Independent Activity:

(20 minutes)

Pass out handout 5.2

We have looked at some general life events as a group, but now let's go inward. Take 10-15 minutes to journal about what your triggers are. Think of 5 situations that you are frequently faced with, and the triggers (internal and external) that are likely to happen for you in those situations.

Plan for how you will manage these triggers. Be specific- instead of saying "call a friend," list out exactly the name of the person in your life that you would call.

Finally, answer the last two prompts:

1. I know I am in a high-risk situation when…

2. I know I can trust myself when….

Group Discussion:

(25-30 minutes)

As with most group discussions we want to focus on group cohesion and support.

Consider going around member by member for this last question. Group members do not have share if they are not ready. A supportive answer to say to the members that share is: "Thank you for sharing."

Let's begin by sharing our findings. What triggers and plans did people come up with?

Prompting Questions as members share:

1. Can anyone relate to those triggers?

2. Are there any blind spots this group member has that anyone is noticing?

3. Does hearing the triggers and plans of one group members inspire anyone in their own situations?

4. What good ideas does group member: _____ have?

Lastly, let's talk about when you know you're in a high-risk situation and how you know you can trust yourself- what did people write?

Closing Statements and Check Out:

(10-15 minutes)

One by one, go around the group and have clients answer the check-out questions.

Pro Tip #3: Write the check-out questions on the board to help the clients remember what is asked.

This group was all about Triggers, and how they can lead to relapse. In today's group we:

1. Explored the role of triggers in relapse.

2. Gained a deeper understanding of what triggers are and how to manage them at events.

3. Identified our personal unique triggers and safety plans for successfully managing them.

Check Out Questions:

1. What is one thing you learned today?

2. How will you implement what you learned?

3. Did you meet your goal set out at the beginning of group?

4. What could have been better about group today?

Event:

List as many triggers and plans for managing the triggers you can think of. Remember to consider: people, places, emotions, sensations, and things

Triggers:	Plan for Managing Triggers:

Triggers in my life and how I will manage them

People:

Places:

Things:

Emotions:

1.   I know I am in a high-risk situation when…

2.   I know I can trust myself when…..

Group Six: Grief

Group topic summary:

Typically, we associate grief with death, however; grief is an experience that can take place when we make both positive or negative changes within our lives. The intention of the group is to educate group members about the grieving process and to normalize the grieving they may be experiencing due to changing their substance use or their mental health. By the end of the group, the goal is that group members are able to label the emotions associated with grief and apply effective coping skills to managing symptoms

Materials: Clients will need some paper, pens and an envelope. There is an option to use a media device to show a YouTube clip.

Length: About 1.5-3 hours (give or take, depending on the group)

Make copies of Handout 6.1 before starting the group.

Check in:

(10 minutes)

Pro Tip #1: Write the check-in prompts up on your board to help the clients remember what info to share.

Pro Tip #2: Write each client's first name and goal up on the board in a place you can return to it later.

Clients go around the room one at a time and check in with the following prompts:

1. How are you feeling today?

2. Did you have any cravings/urges last night (and if so, how did you overcome them)?

3. What is your goal today for group?

Introduction to Topic:

Today we are talking all about grief. We usually think about grief in terms of death, but the truth is we grieve several things in our lives especially when we are experiencing changes. We are going to explore what grief actually is, and the ways it may be manifesting within your lives. We will learn about secondary grief, and how to feel hope throughout life transitions.

Group Discussion:

(10 minutes)

Clients will usually connect with the idea that they may be grieving the loss of their substance of choice, or of the illusion of having a "normal" mental health experience.

The second question introduces the foundation that we grieve changes alongside losses.

The death of a dream is a major element to grief. When we actively move through grief, we are working through resolving our emotions regarding the past, present, and future of the topic. The death of a dream speaks to the grieving of a future that will no longer happen.

Prompting Questions:

1.Why do you think we might be discussing grief in substance abuse (or mental health) focused group?

2. How do you feel you cope with changes in your life, both positive and negative?

3. Can anyone relate to the feeling of grieving the "death of a dream"?

Group Brainstorm:

(20 minutes)

You may have to begin giving clients some examples to support them in finding answers.

Pretty much anything goes here within this umbrella, clients may describe situations such as "wanting to be alone," write the phrases as the clients say them.

Emotions/words to consider:

Anger, sadness, isolation, numbness, irritability, fatigue, wanting to be alone, wanting to never be alone, cravings, fear, guilt, something is missing, strange, different.

Flow straight into group discussion

In this brainstorm we are learning about the emotions that may be manifestations of grief.

Draw an umbrella on the board. In the umbrella write the word Grief.

Prompt clients to shout-out the emotions they feel may fall under the "umbrella" of grief as you write them on the board.

Example:

Group Discussion:

(10-15 minutes)

This group discussion is all about cultivating self-compassion for the emotions the clients may be experiencing. They are likely having all of the emotions under the umbrella happen in waves throughout the day.

Prompting questions:

1. Can anyone share their experiences with the emotions above?

2. Do the emotions show up one at a time, or can multiple emotions be present at the same time? If so, in what ways can that be confusing?

3. When these emotions show up, would you automatically connect them to grief?

4. What happens when we try to make other meanings of the emotions?

Question #4 introduces the concept that we are "meaning making machines"- that we will often feel an emotion, and try to search for (or create) a matching life experience. This can result in confusion and feeling like several things are "wrong." We want to promote the client's ability to discern between a genuine reaction emotion vs. an underlying grief emotion.

Break Time:

(10 minutes)

Group Activity:

(20-30 minutes)

Note: this can be adapted to "Mental Health Diagnosis" as the middle circle where clients then identify what they lost with the diagnosis.

In this discussion, we are normalizing why the clients may be experiencing all of the grief-related emotions.

Group members benefit greatly from having the experience of naming the secondary losses together as it creates group fusion and an environment of mutual understanding.

Allow group members to take a picture of the bubbles (as long as there is nothing identifiable on the board that would compromise confidentiality). They can refer back to the picture if they need reminding of the legitimacy of their emotions.

Big changes are like rocks thrown into a still pond- they create ripples. Secondary losses are the ripples of the pond within our lives. They are the losses that occur due to the primary loss or change.

On the board, create a circle in the middle of the board and write inside of it: "Loss of Drug of Choice."

Have clients go up to the board and write more bubbles around the main bubble in order to demonstrate the extent of the losses with one change.

Example:

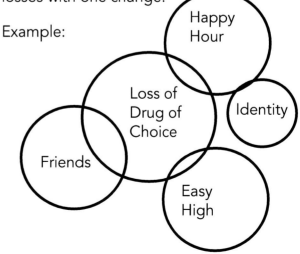

1. What do you think when you look at all of the secondary losses?

2. Did you realize how much was changing in your life with getting sober?

3. Did these factors initially impact the decision to pursue recovery?

Information Session:

(15-20 minutes)

We are reviewing the stages of grief to help clients gain a deeper understanding of the process of grieving.

Grief is not linear. We can feel many emotions at the same time, and we can move "forward" and "backward" hour by hour, day by day.

Clients may want to control their progression through each grief stage. Unfortunately, that tends to set a client up for "failure" as various experiences will trigger the emotions of grief and we cannot fully control whether that happens, and we will often move forward and backward in the stages.

Facilitating the grief process means that we create the environment for grief. If we create the environment, the body and mind will "do their thing" to flow through the experiences naturally.

Some examples:

Journal, listen to music, quiet-time, yoga, go for a walk, un-follow triggering social medias, un-plug from technology, individual therapy,

We are going to look at the stages of grief next:

If you have a media device, google "Giraffe goes through stages of grief/response to change by Dr. Red Shoe" to show to the group.

(If you do not have a media device you can skip the YouTube clip.)

Most of us have heard of the stages of grief: What are they?

Hand out worksheet 6.1

You'll notice that the stages are not in a numbered order or a straight line- why do you think that is?

The worksheet demonstrates the key experience of grief and depicts the circular and up and down nature in which we move into acceptance.

Ask the group if there are any questions about the stages that you can clarify the meaning for (such as bargaining).

We cannot *control* the grief process.

Instead:

We look to *facilitate* the grief process.

We look to create a *flow* of being able to

paint, draw, talk to a friend, meditation.

Prompt clients to explore where they can incorporate healing activities and surroundings into their daily routine.

move through the emotions. If we block the emotions of grief, we can become trapped with unresolved emotions that manifest in our lives overtime.

What activities and surroundings create a flowing healthy environment for the grief emotions to run through?

(Write on the board as group members shout them out)

Final statement: your job as group members is to support one another through the grieving process through accountability and understanding.

Group Activity:

(20-30 minutes)

Now we are doing the opposite of focusing on what we lost, and instead focusing on what we gained.

Write around the main circle what you gained from "losing your drug of choice"

Example:

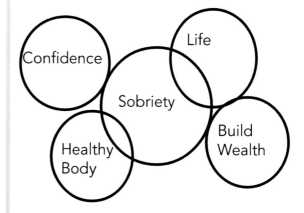

1. How do you feel now after seeing examples of what you lost AND what you gained?

Remember: when we move through the difficulties of grief, we open up space for opportunity and hope.

Final Independent Activity:

(20 minutes)

Clients are given time to write a goodbye letter to their substance of choice.

Some clients may have already tried this activity. If that is the case, there is another option for clients to write a letter to their future self- perhaps highlighting their hopes, well wishes, and a snapshot of where they feel they are currently.

Let's support your grieving process by writing a Goodbye Letter to your substance of choice. You have about 10-15 minutes to write your letter.

Once you're finished with your letter, put it in the envelope provided and seal it. Open up your envelope in 3-6 months.

Closing Statements and Check Out:

(10-15 minutes)

One by one, go around the group and have clients answer the check-out questions.

Pro Tip #3: Write the check-out questions on the board to help the client-s remember what is asked.

This group was all about Grief and the inherent grief response when we make major changes in our lives:

1. Experienced what grief is and the emotions that encompass grief.

2. Explored the grief cycle.

3. Focused on hope for the future.

4. Said goodbye to our substance of choice.

Check Out Questions:

1. What is one thing you learned today?

2. How will you implement what you learned?

3. Did you meet your goal set out at the beginning of group?

4. What could have been better about group today?

Stages of Grief

Acceptance

Adjustment

New Strengths

New Normal

Upward Turn

Hope

Emotional Outbursts

New People

Guilt

Helping Others

Disorganization

Bargaining

Fear

Anger

Denial

Group Seven: Active Listening

Group topic summary:

This group topic is within the category of communication techniques. Healthy communication within relationships requires the skill set of listening to others, as well as being able to advocate to others how we want them to listen to us. When group therapy ends, clients can ideally transfer the emotional intimacy experienced in group into their personal relationships. Active listening can be one of the cornerstones of building such intimacy. By the end of the group, the goal is that group members gain better understanding of how to apply active listening techniques in their daily communication with others. A secondary goal is that clients also gain the insight and vocabulary to successfully ask for others to apply actively listening within their relationships.

Materials: Clients will need some paper, pens and coloring materials

Length: About 1.5-3 hours (give or take, depending on the group)

Make copies of Handouts 7.1-7.11 before starting the group.

Check in:

(10 minutes)

Pro Tip #1: Write the check-in prompts up on your board to help the clients remember what info to share.

Pro Tip #2: Write each client's first name and goal up on the board in a place you can return to it later.

Clients go around the room one at a time and check in with the following prompts:

1. How are you feeling today?

2. Did you have any cravings/urges last night (and if so, how did you overcome them)?

3. What is your goal today for group?

Introduction to Topic:

Today we are going to explore the concept of active listening. It seems simple but there can be a lot that goes into it. Sometimes we can intuitively apply active listening, but usually, we are in the habit of not really listening. This group topic has the ability to create major positive changes in every area of your life in which you interact with others. (Think: intimate relationships, work-life, family, this group!). Active Listening is a tool that you will find yourself using over and over again

Group Discussion:

(10 minutes)

This "pop quiz" usually makes group members laugh. Some groups will repeat it back to you all the way, but usually you'll get a mixed result of half of the group members admitting they weren't listening at all.

As the facilitator, this probably won't offend you, because on some level we have accepted that sometimes people barely listen to us. It helps to normalize this with the clients!

Active listening is a useful tool as it helps us build strong relationships, as well as get our needs met and meet the needs of others who we care about. Both of which are essential

Warm Up Question (pop quiz style!):

So who was really listening to the introduction? Can anyone repeat it back to me?

Prompting Questions:

1. Why is Active Listening likely to be a useful tool when it comes to mental health and recovery?

2. Where did you learn your habits when it comes to listening, does this effect you today?

3. How can active listening improve your connections to others?

when it comes to rebuilding or strengthening different relationships during recovery.

Many group members first learned about how to actively listening from their parents or their early teachers. Usually, by trying to trying to teach them how to follow directions. Typically, "not listening" brought about some sort of "punishment" (bad grades, detention, time-out). As a result, just the words "Active Listening" can frustrate group members.

Here we introduce active listening for connection instead of just to "follow directions". We want to empower clients to make stronger connections with others in their lives.

*Social media can have a huge role on active listening! Often, we are so bombarded with information from others that we get really used to tuning out.

4. How does Social Media effect active listening in these modern days?

Group Activity[1]:

(35-45 minutes)

This group activity is a fun way to introduce the application of active listening. Group members typically listen very intently during this exercise, and it leads to an enjoyable group discussion following the activity.

Turn to figures 7.1-7.10.

Make copies of these images to pass out to clients

1. Put clients in groups of 2, and have them sit back to back. Determine who will instruct and who will draw first.

(If you have more than 10 clients in the group, look online for a scene of a cartoon to use. If you have less that 4 clients in the group, you can read the picture out and the clients can all draw at once together)

2. Set a timer for 10 minutes and pass out the first round of images at random to the group member "instructing" first in each group.

3. Instructions: The group member instructing must describe to the group member drawing the image with as much detail as possible. The group member

drawing has to do their best to interpret what the instructor is saying and recreate the picture just from the verbal instruction they hear. No hand gestures allowed, but members can ask each other questions.

4. At the end, we will compare the client's drawing to the real image and then switch.

5. Pass out new pictures to the new instructors.

Group Discussion:

(35-45 minutes)

Now we will process the activity and the implications of it in the real world.

Feel free to "round-robin" (aka ask everyone one at a time) the group members to get them to answer this first question!

Here in the discussion we reinforce active listening for the purpose of connection, group members were simply talking and listening, but usually feel closer after the activity. This is because it's fun, and we can really connect to others we feel are paying attention to us.

Prompting Questions:

1. How did that activity go for everyone?

2. Did anyone feel frustrated? How did you handle it?

3. Do you listen this closely all the time when others are talking to you?

4. What did this activity show you about your communication abilities (listening and instructing)?

5. Do you feel closer to the group member that you were paired with? If so, why? Or- why not?

Break Time:

(10 minutes)

Information Session [2]:

(15-20 minutes)

Poor Active Listening examples: No eye-contact, looking at your phone while talking, interrupting, etc.

Before we get into the properties of good Active Listening, what are the signs of poor Active Listening?

This is where we get into the details of what active listening actually is and how to apply it.

Physical Signs:

- Eye contact
- Matching their body language
- Nodding your head along
- Facial expressions

Paraphrasing:

Restating back to the person speaking facts of what they said:

- "So I am hearing that what happened was…"
- Interpret back to the speaker what you heard them say.

Reflecting:

This is when we reflect back to the speaker their feelings about what they said. It helps validate a person:

- "It sounds like you feel…."
- Shows understanding of how the other person feels.
- "I understand feeling…."

Clarifying:

Get more information from the speaker
- Elicit more information
- "What you are saying is that you….?"
- "Am I correct about…?"
- "Can you say that in a different way?"

Encouraging

This is where we show interest by saying:

- "Tell me more!"
- "Really?!"
- "What happened next?"

Write on the board and allow group members to shout out examples of each while you scribe:

1. Physical signs of Active Listening

How do you know verbally when people are listening? We are only going to focus on the top 4 common cues for active listening:

1. Paraphrasing
2. Reflecting
3. Clarifying
4. Encouraging

Bonus:

1. Texting

The circle below demonstrates the Communication Model and what sends the most information to others when we communicate. Consider that with texting: *all we have are words.*

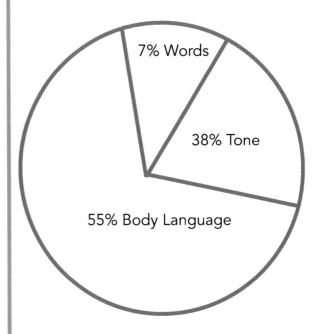

Keep this info up on the board for the duration of the group

Virtual Listening (texting)

- If you aren't able to focus at this time: "This sounds really important, can we talk about it in person or on the phone?
- I'm reading that you are saying...
- Clarifying is more important than ever considering how much is lost in translation with texting
- Not replying to feeling statements with a meme.

Group Activity:

(20 minutes)

Hold the time for each discussion.

Depending on the time, you can also prompt the groups of 2 to demonstrate being a bad listeners for one minute before practicing good listening.

Break up into small groups of 2.

Take turns (about 10 minutes each) telling the other person a story about your life or day. The story needs to be real yet be mindful of your wellbeing with disclosing any trauma experiences.

The listener needs to use at least FIVE (5) of the techniques listed on the board to practice active listening.

Group Discussion:

(15 minutes)

Common answers could include shutting down, or getting angry. The use of active listening when there is a difference in opinion allows us the ability to better understand the other's point of view, and to de-escalate any conflict emotions.

Active Listening brings several benefits into our lives. Especially, in times of conflict or disagreement:

1. How do you typically handle it if others have a different opinion from your own?

2. Can you see someone else's view as also correct?

3. How does active listening help you with managing the difference/conflict?

Independent Activity:

(15 minutes)

Fill out the worksheet (Handout 7.11) about integrating active listening into your own life.

Closing Statements and Check Out:

(10-15 minutes)

One by one, go around the group and have clients answer the check-out questions.

Pro Tip #3: Write the check-out questions on the board to help the clients remember what is asked.

This group was all about Active Listening, and the role it plays in our recovery and mental health stability. In this group we:

1. Experienced what active listening is and where it can be useful.

2. Practiced our own versions of active listening.

3. Explored how active listening can also be a tool for conflict resolution.

4. Planned for integrating the information into our personal lives.

Check Out Questions:

1. What is one thing you learned today?

2. How will you implement what you learned?

3. Did you meet your goal set out at the beginning of group?

4. What could have been better about group today?

Figure 7.1

Figure 7.2

Figure 7.3

Figure 7.4

Figure 7.5

Figure 7.6

Figure 7.7

Figure 7.8

Figure 7.9

Figure 7.10

Active Listening in My Life

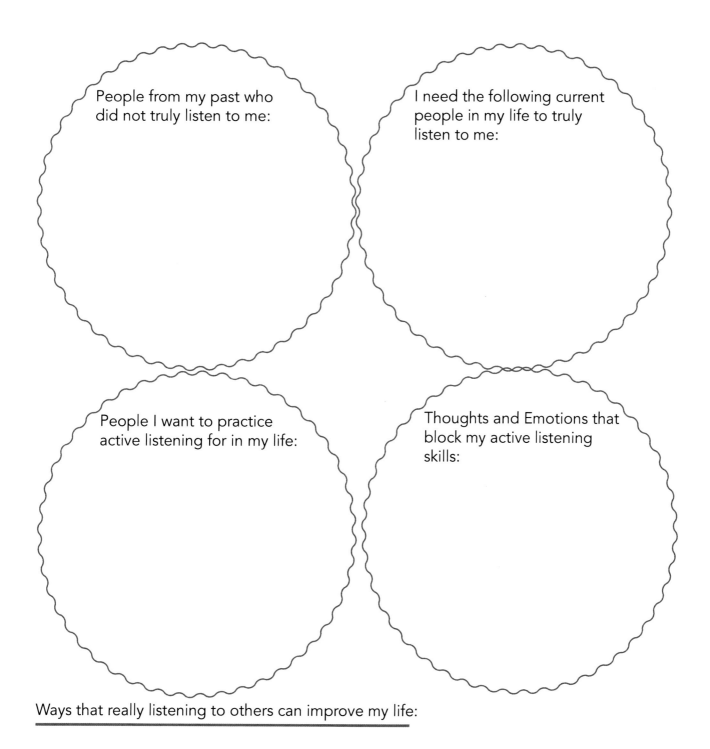

People from my past who did not truly listen to me:

I need the following current people in my life to truly listen to me:

People I want to practice active listening for in my life:

Thoughts and Emotions that block my active listening skills:

Ways that really listening to others can improve my life:

Sources

[1] Adapted from Exercise 4.2.1, Creating a Culture of Peace in the English Language Classroom by Alison Milofsky (United States Institute of Peace).

[2] Global Peace Building Center, United States Institute of Peace. Retrieved on Oct 7, 2019: https://www.usip.org/public-education/educators/lessons-and-activities

(Images Sourced using Envato Elements with full licensing and permission)

Group Eight: The Hero's Journey

Group topic summary:

The intention of the group topic is to bring awareness and attention to the cycles of triumph and difficulty in life. This group is designed to normalize the client's experience of life overall and to prompt them to view themselves as the hero of their story. By the end of the group, the goal is that group members will have awareness of where they believe they are in their journey and how they can empower themselves to keep moving forward.

Materials: Clients will need some post-its, paper, and pens.

Length: About 1.5-3 hours (give or take, depending on the group)

Make copies of Handout 8.1 before starting the group.

Check in:

(10 minutes)

Pro Tip #1: Write the check-in prompts up on your board to help the clients remember what info to share.

Pro Tip #2: Write each client's first name and goal up on the board in a place you can return to it later.

Clients go around the room one at a time and check in with the following prompts:

1. How are you feeling today?

2. Did you have any cravings/urges last night (and if so, how did you overcome them)?

3. What is your goal today for group?

Introduction to Topic:

Today we are going to dive into learning more about the Hero's Journey as a concept and how to apply it to your current life circumstance. This is one (of many) ways you can conceptualize life and what you're going through. As always, group topics are about finding what works best for you and there are no "one-size-fits-all" answers. I think today's topic is a really unique and relatable way to process life's difficulties.

Brief Education:

(20 minutes)

Read through the stages together

Hand out Worksheet 8.1 which demonstrates the hero's journey and the accompanying description of each stage.

Prompting questions:

Are any stories/movies coming to mind that demonstrate this journey?

What is you favorite story of a Hero's Journey?

Group Discussion

(30 minutes)

Clients will identify what their journey is about (for example: Getting Sober) and then identify themselves to a particular stage. Give group members about 10 minutes to complete this step.

On the worksheet provided, note where you are in your hero's journey and fill in the blanks associated with your journey.

Discussion Questions:

1. Where are you on the journey?

2. Tell us about how you relate to the hero's journey.

3. What do you remember about the previous steps before where you are now?

4. What emotions might go along with each step?

5. How can you show yourself compassion for wherever you are?

6. What might make a person give up before the journey is complete?

7. What do you think happens if a hero gives up?

Break Time:

(10 minutes)

Group Activity:

(30-40 minutes)

We are using the journey of "getting sober" as an example for this guide. You can choose another journey that the group members have in common.

Give group members each a stack of sticky notes.

Let's say we are all on the hero's journey of getting sober.

Draw 4 squares on the board and write the following in each square:

1. Hero

2. Guide

3. Dark Cave

4. Treasure

Take your time going through each quadrant and discussing the things that come up for the clients. This is a good opportunity for group cohesion (can anyone relate to what ____ said?) and for empowering clients to keep going on the journey.

Examples:

1. Hero: Me, This Group

2. Guides: Therapy, AA, my family

3. Dark Cave: Relapse, giving up, embracing trauma

4. Treasure: Spending time with children again

1.Let's look at the hero first. In the "getting sober" journey who is the hero? Write down some options on your sticky note and stick it up on the board in the hero section.

We're going to repeat this for each step:

2. When you think of the guides on this journey of getting sober- who or what could that be for you?

3. What experiences and processes could the "Dark Cave" of getting sober?

4. What are the treasures that you will receive for your success in this journey?

Are there any final thoughts about this process?

Independent Activity:

(15-20 minutes)

We are going to spend the rest of our time together today with an independent activity before moving into the check-out.

On your piece of paper, write a letter to yourself for the Dark Cave.

Remember, the Dark Cave is when you surrender. Imagine what that time will feel like for you and write yourself the letter you might need to read if the Dark Cave stage comes your way.

Closing Statements and Check Out:

(10-15 minutes)

One by one, go around the group and have clients answer the check-out questions.

Pro Tip #3: Write the check-out questions on

This group was all about The Hero's Journey and how it applies to our life. In this group we:

1. Learned about the Hero's Journey.

2. Explored the emotions, experiences, and the stages of the journey.

3. Applied the Hero's Journey to our own lives and where we are currently.

the board to help the clients remember what is asked.

4. Practiced self-compassion through letter writing for ourselves in our next "Dark Cave".

Check Out Questions:

1. What is one thing you learned today?

2. How will you implement what you learned?

3. Did you meet your goal set out at the beginning of group?

4. What could have been better about group today?

Return as a
new person

Discomfort rises and the Hero
says YES to the journey

The Gift/
Treasure

Start

The Hero's
Journey

Changes

Team up/
guides arrive

Revelation

Trials &
Tribulations

Death/Dark
Cave

The Hero's Journey Steps:

1. Start: Discomfort starts brewing in your life and you feel compelled to take action. Doors open for you and opportunities present themselves. Meanwhile, "staying the same" feels increasingly uncomfortable and like less of an option. As a result, you say "Yes" to the call to adventure!

2. Teaming Up/Guides: Jumping into the unknown is scary. You will usually need the help of someone else. You "team up" with people who will be there to support you on the journey- or at least get you started on your way.

3. Trials and Tribulations: The tough stuff starts, and you feel stressed, worn, and beaten down. You get through some initial battles, and think you might be finally moving forward, until you get knocked back down again. It takes all you have to keep fighting.

4. Death/Dark Cave: You will experience failure and stress like you've never seen before- you hit rock bottom. You surrender to your dark cave. You think this is the end for you, and that you may not survive it. You surrender.

5. Revelation: You realize what you needed has been within you all along. You then harness what you learned about yourself and the world during your rock bottom. You have the answer.

6. Changes: You implement the changes into your life. You are changed. You have come out of the other side of the journey.

7. The Gift/Treasure: You are rewarded for your journey. You receive the gift that you have rightfully fought to receive.

8. Return as a new person: You resume your day to day life in society, forever changed by your experience. You offer what you learned to others in your community.

Life is a series of hero's journeys. We get a small period of time in-between journeys, and we expect that homeostasis to be everlasting. However, the cycle continues and we are called to adventure over and over again.

Sources

The Hero's Journey is a concept originally developed by Joseph Campbell. The Hero's Journey was adapted for the purposes of this group. You can read more about the origin of the Hero's Journey in Joseph Campbell's book, "The Hero's Journey: Joseph Campbell on His Life and Work (The Collected Works of Joseph Campbell)".

Group Nine: Boundaries

Group topic summary:

This group topic focuses on helping group members learn about boundaries and how to hold healthy boundaries. By the end of the group, the goal is that group members gain greater awareness into their current boundary styles and feel empowered in their ability to set healthy boundaries with others.

Materials: Clients will need some paper and a pen.

Length: About 1.5-3 hours (give or take, depending on the group)

Make copies of Handouts 9.3 and 9.4 before starting the group.

Check in:

(10 minutes)

Pro Tip #1: Write the check-in prompts up on your board to help the clients remember what info to share.

Pro Tip #2: Write each client's first name and goal up on the board in a place you can return to it later.

Clients go around the room one at a time and check in with the following prompts:

1. How are you feeling today?

2. Did you have any cravings/urges last night (and if so, how did you overcome them)?

3. What is your goal today for group?

Introduction to Topic:

Today is all about boundaries. What they are and how to apply them! Healthy boundaries are essential to our wellbeing and they can be frequently tested. Sometimes they can slip without us realizing. In this group we are going to focus on being more intentional with our boundaries and aware of maintaining healthy boundaries as we heal.

Group Activity:

(30 minutes)

A Day in a Boundary-less Life

Pro Tip #3: You know your group best! Consider what kind of attention span your group has. You can read the story all the way through and discuss, or pick stopping points to pause and discuss.

Read out loud to the group the story found in handout 9.1

As you read, ask group members to either jot down or pay close attention to where there is a boundary issue in the story.

What boundary violations did the group catch?

Group Discussion:

(30 minutes)

There are many different points to process in the discussion of _A day in a Boundary-less Life_.

See Handout 9.2 for a cheat sheet of boundary violations.

Clients will have several reactions to the story, take time to process and normalize the client's reactions.

Prompting Questions:

1. Are any thoughts coming up for the group about Mary's life?

2. What unhealthy boundaries did you notice?

3. What do you think about Mary's relationships with Ted and Trisha?

4. Do you think Mary's relationships with Ted and Trisha are doomed or can they be helped with some boundaries?

5. What emotions were you feeling on Mary's behalf when you listened to the story?

6. What do you think will happen for Mary in the future?

7. Does Mary's story seem unrealistic?

Break Time:

(10 minutes)

Group Brainstorm:

(10 minutes)

Brainstorm together about unhealthy and healthy boundaries. The previous story will have started the process of identifying boundaries.

Allow group members to brain storm and shout out answers. Here are some examples to get you started:

Unhealthy:

• Trusting everyone or trusting no one

What are some examples of unhealthy boundaries?

• Not knowing the difference between appropriate & inappropriate comments and behaviors
• Talking about very personal information with someone when you first meet
• Violating your own values for someone else
• Love at first sight (This can be a good factor to debate)
• Touch without permission
• Letting other people decide what your boundaries will be
• Abuse of any kind (physical, sexual, emotional, financial)
• Putting someone else's needs before your own
• Spending money you don't have

Healthy:

• Focusing on your own needs
• Saying "No"
• Having awareness of when your own boundaries are being crossed
• Healthy, mutually satisfying relationships
• Asking to touch or be touched
• Communicating clearly
• Allowing intimacy with friends and lovers to grow slowly
• Knowing yourself
• Trusting yourself

What are some examples of healthy boundaries?

Information Session:

(20 minutes)

See handout for examples for each

Brainstorm together on what each boundary type might mean before giving out answers

There are different types of boundaries. Let's explore them together.

(Handout 9.3 page 1)

1. Rigid Boundary
2. No Boundary
3. Partial Boundary
4. Healthy Boundary

Examples:

"This is what I need"

"That is unacceptable"

"No Thank you"

"Yes, I do mind"

"I am uncomfortable sharing more at this time"

"Perhaps later as we get to know each other more"

"I am unable to talk at this time, I will check in with you later"

Communicating our healthy boundaries can feel difficult.

Let's practice by going over what Mary could have said.

Go back to the boundary violations observed earlier and practice as a group how Mary could have communicated healthy boundaries.

Individual Activity:

(30 minutes)

Allow clients to answer the questions independently.

Changing boundaries can be tough! People push-back, sometimes relationships have to end. Clients may need support with the difficulties they identify.

Ask clients to get their paper and pen out and answer the following prompts independently:

(Handout 9.4)

1. People and places in my life that I need to establish healthy boundaries with are:

2. I need better boundaries with myself about:

3. Some boundaries I can implement today are:

4. Benefits of changing my boundaries:

5. Difficulties I may experience changing my boundaries:

Group Discussion:

(20 minutes)

Ask the group to share their answers to each question, leaving time for feedback for the client's answers.

Statements to foster group participation:

Can anyone relate?

Did anyone else have that on their list?

How can we help you?

We want to help the group with the understanding that we seek progress, not perfection. There is no such thing as perfection, even when it comes to boundaries. With self-awareness, we can see where boundaries are slipping, and we constantly adjust our communication to put boundaries back in place.

This is a pro-active question. Sometimes if we are tired, hungry, lonely, or busy our boundaries can slip. This is also true if our mental health declines. When we become aware of big changes in our lives, we need to be extra aware of the boundaries we are keeping with others.

Final Discussion Questions:

Is it possible to have perfect boundaries?

What factors might make us lose self-awareness of our boundaries?

Closing Statements and Check Out:

(10-15 minutes)

One by one, go around the group and have clients answer the check-out questions.

Pro Tip #4: Write the check-out questions on the board to help the clients remember what is asked.

This group was an introduction to boundaries. We covered:

1. How boundaries play out in a day-to-day experience.
2. The difference between healthy and unhealthy boundaries.
3. The four types of boundaries.
4. How to communicate boundaries effectively.
5. Ways to implement into our own lives.

Check Out Questions:

1. What is one thing you learned today?
2. How will you implement what you learned?
3. Did you meet your goal set out at the beginning of group?
4. What could have been better about group today?

A Day in a Boundary-less Life

6AM

Mary wakes with a jolt to the shrill sound of her alarm. "How is it already time to wake up?" she mutters to herself. "Oh yeah, I'm up early to finish my final marketing presentation by the 9AM meeting. Ugh."

She quietly rolls out of bed, careful as to not to wake her husband, Ted, as he is never in a good mood in the mornings. Aware that she still has a lot of work to do on her presentation, she gets dressed and ready as quickly as possible. Just when she reaches for her door to head downstairs and start working, she hears a grunt from Ted.

"Mary! Can you bring me coffee? And what about making those eggs you made yesterday?" Ted grumbles, still half asleep.

Mary replies, "Ted, I'm just… well, I'm just a little busy this mor---"

Ted interrupts, "Mary! Please! I need it!"

"Okay" Mary says, I'll get it ready for you.

6:45AM

Mary quickly pours the coffee and flips the eggs on the stove. Feeling, flustered, she reassures herself, "It's okay, I still have a good hour or so to finish up my work". Suddenly, the phone rings.

"Good morning, Mary!" she hears loud and clear through the speaker of her phone. "It's your mother calling, I'm so happy I caught you… I have a big favor to ask, I know it's a lot, but if you love me… you will understand."

"What is it?" Mary asks with hesitation…

"Well, I was thinking it's time to redecorate my living room and I'm willing to give you anything in there that I end up replacing, but I need you to come over tonight and help me move around the furniture."

Mary's stomach drops as she remembers that she signed up for a yoga class tonight after work that she will get charged for if she tries to cancel this late. She really wants to go to the class, but what kind of daughter doesn't help her mother when she calls? Mary sighs as she says, "Sure, mom. I'll be there around 6."

"I knew I could depend on you!" Mary's mother exclaims, "You're just the best. See you later!"

Mary glances over to the eggs on the stove "Ugh. I totally forgot about the eggs!" She grimaces as she tries to slide the eggs off the pan and realizes they are burnt to a crisp.

7AM

Ted plods into the kitchen, "Oh Mary! My eggs!"

"I know" Mary replies, "mom called, and I got distracted and well…" Mary looks up to see Ted's face, furrowed with disappointment.

"I'll just re-make them. Don't worry." Mary reassures Ted.

Ted replies, "That feels like the right decision to me. Thanks, Mary."

7:45AM

Mary sits down with her presentation. She has to leave for work at 8:30, but she tells herself she can focus and just get the presentation completed as best as she can. She opens up her computer and starts typing rapidly.

8:15AM

Thirty minutes into working on her presentation, Mary feels like she is on a roll. Suddenly her phone lights up. Mary looks at her screen to see an Instagram notification come through: Doug the Pug has posted a new video. Mary loves Doug the Pug. She thinks to herself, "I'll just watch this one video, and then get back to work, Doug the Pug always makes me happy so it's probably good for my mood to see his latest post."

8:37AM

Mary glances to the time on her phone. "Arghhh! I'm late!" Mary quickly puts her phone in her purse and slams her laptop shut. It seems she got side tracked scrolling through Instagram. "What kind of time-warp was that?" she wonders to herself. Then she realizes, "Maybe I didn't have time to sign up for that smoothie delivery add I saw on instagram, but it just seemed like such a good deal."

Running out to her car, she speeds to the metro station.

9AM

Waiting on the platform for the train, she looks at her phone again. An overdraft notice from her bank pops up. Mary logs into her bank and stares despondently at her account. Ted ordered several things on Amazon yesterday. She asked him to wait until her paycheck went through, but it looks like he couldn't wait. The smoothie delivery she just purchased pushed her into over-draft. For a split second, Mary thinks about calling Ted and asking him to cancel his Amazon order. She stops herself by thinking, "Well, I should have checked my balance before ordering my smoothie thing anyway- this is my fault". She decides the overdraft fee will just have to be something she pays.

10AM

Mary arrives to work an hour late. She could have made it in earlier, but she missed her first train when a group of tourists cut in front of her on the platform. She hung back when the train arrived as to not rush them as they boarded. She was lost in thought when her boss, Natalie, tapped her on shoulder.

"Mary. You're late. You are an hour late and I am getting worried this is becoming a habit." Natalie scolded, "We started the meeting without you and I decided to have Jan run your presentation, can you send her your slides?"

"Sure" Mary sadly replies.

Natalie defends herself as she walks away, "You leave me no choice, Mary."

Mary sits down at her desk and answers e-mails as they come through. Mary works in the marketing department and there is always work to be done, but she doesn't get to most of it.

Somehow, she finds that she has become the point person for organizing her co-worker's baby shower. She estimates that she gets about 20 e-mails a day from people asking for details about the shower. She sighs to herself as she says, "Why won't they just check the invitation for these details? It's all there! Then I wouldn't have to answer everyone individually."

12PM

"MARY!" Shouts Trisha. "Lunch time?!"

Trisha sits in the cubicle next to Mary. She is very out-going and likes to talk. Mary and Trisha have lunch most days of the week. Mary was hoping to relax over her lunch break today, yet automatically replies, "Sure Trisha. That sounds great! Can we go to the cafeteria? I packed my lunch today so I can just eat that while you buy something."

"Ewe" Trisha replies. "I'm not getting cafeteria food. Just leave your sad packed lunch and let's get sushi."

Sometimes Mary's stomach reacts to raw fish, but she agrees that sushi would be fine.

While at the sushi joint, Trisha starts to tell Mary all about her recent dating escapades. Mary starts to shift around uncomfortably. She thinks to herself, "I really want to support Trisha, but she just tells me so many details about her life when we are only co-workers."

Trisha is finishing up on her gossip when she asks Mary a very personal question, "Mary, what's going on with you and Ted? Sometimes I can tell you aren't happy- tell me everything."

Mary flushes and stutters, "Well, Trisha, no… everything is fine, I'm just not feeling appreciated, that's all."

"Not appreciated about what? I need details." Trisha replies.

Mary's mind starts to spin from anxiety. It is true, she has been feeling sad about Ted lately, but she has not even processed it yet herself. She doesn't feel ready to talk about it with ether people, especially Trisha. Mary wonders if she can quickly cover-up the anxiety and just say the bare minimum.

Mary blurts out, "Okay Trisha the truth is, I do everything in the house, he does nothing. He spends our money without considering me, and he never asks how my day is going." That was not the bare minimum Mary had in mind.

"Oooo" Trisha replied.

Mary felt hot with embarrassment. "Trisha does not actually care about this or me" Mary realized, "I just gave her a lot of office gossip to spread around".

Trisha, noticing Mary's anxiety, quickly replies, "Listen Mary, I'm going to order us some drinks. Just a little lunch time relaxer, nothing major. I can tell you need a little pick-me-up."

The last thing Mary wants to do is drink in the middle of the day. However, she is feeling so uncomfortable with her anxiety and embarrassment. "Okay" Mary replies automatically. She rationalizes the choice by thinking to herself, "If I'm going to be stuck here with Trisha, maybe a drink is necessary."

Trisha orders two glasses of wine and drinks hers quickly. Mary has only had a few bites of her food when the check arrives. Trisha reaches over and grabs the remaining sushi rolls on Mary's plate and eats them in one bite. "You've got the check this time, right?" Trisha looks at Mary expectantly. "I forgot my wallet at the office- I can just get our check at the next lunch."

Mary agrees and pulls out her "emergency fund" savings card to pay for the meal. She doesn't want Trisha to see her usual card get declined due to being in overdraft. Mary's heart sinks when she looks at the check and sees that the wine Trisha ordered costs $31.00 a glass, bringing the total bill to $121.

5PM

Mary's afternoon passes by without much work being completed. Trisha kept interrupting her to show her memes or gossip. Mary was hoping Trisha would leave her alone because she had her headphones in, but it seems they went unnoticed.

She rides the train home and gets off at the stop nearest to her mom's house. She wishes she was headed to yoga, but since the raw fish from the sushi is not sitting well in her stomach, she rationalizes to herself, "I couldn't have made it through yoga anyway."

The nearest train stop to mom's house is still a $15 Uber ride away. Mary pays the Uber driver and tips extra. She's not sure why she tipped, as the driver mostly talked her ear off about himself… but she didn't want to hurt his feelings. She considers next time asking mom to pick her up, but Mary knows her mom does not like to spend money on gas.

6PM

Mary is moving furniture around at her mom's house, while her mom observes her from the sunroom. "Thank you, Mary!" her mom shouts over to her. "I was going to ask your dad to help with this task, but you know how he doesn't like to do chores after a hard work day."

Mary wants to explode with anger when she hears her mom say this about her dad. "Does she think I like to do chores after a work day?" she exclaims under her breath.

"What was that, dear?" Mary's mom asked.

"Nothing!" Mary replies. "Mom, can you get the other side of this table?"

"I'm just too comfortable to move" her mom replies, "Just leave it where it is, this is not urgent anyway."

Mary finishes up what she can when she glances at the clock. "Mom, it's 7:15PM! I need to get home to Ted. The last train leaves at 7:45 and I don't want to miss it."

"Before you go, listen to what Barb told me today at the plant store…" Mary's mom interrupts. She goes into a story that Mary is too distracted to pay attention to. Mary finds herself nodding along while glancing at the clock every minute. The clock ticks to 7:44 and Mary realizes she has already missed the last train.

"Okay mom, I really have to go." Mary says as she calls an Uber and pays $45 for the Uber to take her all the way back to her house across town.

8PM

Mary walks into the house and finds the kitchen to be a mess. It seems Ted made himself spaghetti, and the remains of it are all over the place. She starts to clean it up as Ted walks in the room.

"Hey Ted, wow… this is quite the mess. Where did you put the spaghetti? I'm starving." Mary asks.

"The spaghetti is in my stomach!" Ted laughs, "I figured you already ate so I finished it all, I'm actually feeling too full if you can believe it."

Mary feels tears welling up. She doesn't want Ted to see her cry so she moves into the pantry and starts eating potato chips. The salty chips distract her from her emotions and she rejoins Ted into the kitchen.

"Let's watch our show!" Ted exclaims.

Watching TV seems to be the only thing Ted and Mary do these days. Mary agrees to watching TV when her phone chimes.

Mary looks down at her phone to see a work e-mail come through from Jan:

Mary, Natalie wants me running the final presentation. I noticed only half of the slides are finished. Can you please finish up and send the rest to me by 9AM tomorrow? I want to have plenty of time over the weekend to practice running through everything.

Mary's heart sinks. "Ted, watch the show without me, I have to finish up some work."

"Sure thing!" Ted replies, "you will be so behind, but that's on you!"

9:45PM

Mary sends the last slide off to Jan. "At least that's over with" she exhales.

Exhausted, Mary gets ready for bed and enters the bedroom to find Ted already falling asleep.

Ted rouses at the sound of Mary entering the room and lifts his head up groggily, "Hey Mary…I need to tell you what happened on our show!" Ted shouts out.

"Okay" Mary replies, knowing she would rather watch the show for herself.

"That last episode was the best, you gotta watch it, they win the war and reunite in the end! It is so good!"

Ted has just spoiled the finale to the last episode of a show Mary has been following for 4 years. Too tired to argue, she climbs into bed and hopes to be able to fall asleep soon.

"Tomorrow's another day" Mary thinks to herself, "Maybe it can be different."

The End.

Cheat Sheet of Boundary Violations

6AM:

1. Mary does not have time to make coffee for Ted. Making coffee for him anyway when she has work to do is an example of where Mary is allowing Ted to cross her boundaries.

6:45 AM:

2. Mary violates her own boundaries by answering her phone when she is busy and has a time-bound activity to complete.

3. Mary agrees to help her mother in the evening and cancel her self-care plans.

4. Mary loses money on the yoga class by cancelling late.

7AM:

5. Mary makes eggs again despite running out of time.

6. Mary violates her own boundaries with herself by checking her phone while she has work to complete.

8:37AM:

7. Mary violates boundaries with herself again by staying on social media for 30 minutes when she has a project to complete.

9AM:

8. Mary allows Ted to violate her boundaries by spending money when they agreed to wait to purchase anything.

9. Mary violates her own boundaries by spending money before her paycheck goes through.

10AM

10. Mary misses her train by allowing tourists to cut her off on the train platform.

11. Mary allows herself to become a point person for the baby shower despite not having enough time to dedicate to the task.

12. Mary individually answers each e-mail instead of redirecting people back to the initial invitation.

12PM:

13. Mary agrees to go to lunch with Trisha despite knowing she does not want to.

14. Trisha violates Mary's boundaries by deciding that Mary will not eat her packed lunch.

15. Mary agrees to Sushi even though it hurts her stomach.

16. Trisha violates Mary's boundaries and her own boundaries by telling Mary intimate information about her life.

17. Mary violates her boundaries by answering the personal information Trisha asked for.

18. Mary allows Trisha to order her a drink despite knowing she does not want a drink.

19. Trisha eats Mary's food without asking

20. Mary pays the check despite not being able to afford it.

5PM:

21. Mary allows Trisha to violate her boundaries all afternoon and relies on her headphones to passively communicate boundaries.

22. Mary pays for an Uber she cannot currently afford to go to her mother's after work.

6PM:

23. Mary does not share her authentic feelings with her mother about moving furniture after a long day at work.

24. Mary misses her train from letting her mother talk to her when she needed to leave.

25. Mary pays for her Uber home, another expense she cannot afford.

8PM:

26. Mary cleans the kitchen without asking for help.

27. Mary eats potato chips instead of expressing her emotions.

28. Mary encourages Ted to watch their show without her.

29. Mary violates her work/life balance boundary by working on the presentation during after-work hours when it is not actually urgent.

9:45PM:

30. Mary allows Ted to violate her boundaries by spoiling her show for her.

Types of Boundaries

Rigid	None

Partial	Healthy

Answer Sheet

Rigid

- Hides or does not acknowledge feelings
- Appears detached or non-interested
- Does not ask for, or accept help
- Does not initiate or allow any physical touch
- Nothing gets in, and nothing gets out
- Can come across as rude

None

- Touches without asking
- Tries not to ever be alone
- Calls and texts even if you say you are busy
- Feels responsible for the feelings of others, and makes you responsible for their feelings
- Tells very personal information right away
- Overcompensates
- Puts others before themselves even when it hurts
- Invades privacy

Partial

- Inconsistent between rigid and no boundaries

- Mood changes/swings

Healthy

- Communicates Clearly
- Asks permission before touching others
- Shares feelings directly
- Aligns actions with values
- Allows for differences between themselves and others
- Allows intimacy to grow slowly in relationships
- Able to say "No"
- When earned, trusts fully
- Respectful to others and themselves
- Maintains Privacy

Handout 9.4

1.People and places in my life that I need to establish healthy boundaries with are:

2. I need better boundaries with myself about:

3. Some boundaries I can implement today are:

4. Benefits of changing my boundaries:

5. Difficulties I may experience changing my boundaries:

Group Ten: Physical Health

Group topic summary:

This group topic focuses on helping group members gain insight into the role that proper nutrition and physical health plays within their overall healing process, and serves as another element to the mind & body connection of recovery. By the end of the group, the goal is that group members experience higher levels of self-awareness about the impact of physical health on their recovery.

Materials: Clients will need some paper, pens and coloring materials

Length: About 1.5-3 hours (give or take, depending on the group)

Make copies of Handout 10.1-10.4 before starting the group.

Disclaimer:

We are not nutritionists or physical trainers! Because we are not licensed nutritionists or trainers, we cannot prescribe specific diets or workouts to our clients or recommend what they eat/do. However, we can provide basic education to what nutrition means and empower clients to use the information to incorporate better self-care with food into their mind & body healing process. We can also motivate clients to take better care of their physical health to support their recovery.

Check in:

(10 minutes)

Pro Tip #1: Write the check-in prompts up on your board to help the clients remember what info to share.

Pro Tip #2: Write each clients first name and goal up on the board in a place you can return to it later.

Clients go around the room one at a time and check in with the following prompts:

1. How are you feeling today?

2. Did you have any cravings/urges last night (and if so, how did you overcome them)?

3. What is your goal today for group?

Introduction to Topic:

Today, we are talking about the role physical health within your recovery. Our physical health has a lot to do with how we feel, and we know recovery can feel pretty rough physically. For our physical health we are going to focus on what we eat and our exercise habits. Physical and mental health are connected. By the end of the group we hope to increase your mind/body connection.

Independent Activity:

(10 minutes)

Have clients fill in what they ate yesterday (or last sober time) into each category. Once this is complete, have them set this aside for later.

To begin to better support our physical health, let's first look at our eating habits:

What did you eat yesterday (or on the last sober day/time of your life you can remember)?

Ask clients to make the following categories on their paper:

4. Breakfast
5. Snacks
6. Lunch
7. Dinner
8. Water Amount:

Group Brainstorm:

(10 minutes)

Common food patterns that arise during active drug or alcohol use:

- **No Breakfast**
- **High amounts of sugar and refined carbohydrates**
- **Processed and/or fast food**
- **Low amounts of protein**
- **Skipping meals**
- **High amounts of dairy**

Now we will look at regular eating habits when you are using or in a mental health decline.

What were/are your eating habits while you were/are using?

Write the Categories on the board and have the group shout out answers to what they ate when they were actively using.

Categories:

Breakfast, Snacks, Lunch, Dinner, Water:

Group Discussion:

(15- 20 minutes)

This is an opportunity for the clients to have a group discussion about their eating patterns now compared to the general patterns established during active use.

The prompting questions in this discussion are geared towards helping the group gain insight into the ways their eating habits have changed (or not changed!), and the impact that might be having on how they are currently feeliing

Following the first group discussion, we will move into more information about nutrition and eating habits for promoting recovery.

Who wants to share their food habits from yesterday (or the last remembered sober day/time)?

Prompting Questions:

1. Compare what we have on the board from eating habits during active use to the log you made of your eating habits when sober; are there major differences between the two? If so, what are you noticing?

2. Has anyone noticed that their eating habits haven't changed much at all?

3. What kind of factors might describe why there have or have not been changes?

Pro Tip #3: Some groups will know the factors instantly. Others may need help connecting what factors have changed. Some common ones to consider: more/less money, time changes, habits are set in stone, living with others now, hungry more often

4. In what ways might your body or mood be affected by what you eat?

Break Time:

(10 minutes)

Information Session and Discussion:

(30 minutes)

The hand outs identify some of the impact of using alcohol and drugs on the body. Once the clients have the handouts, give them some time to read through them while you read the major points quickly out loud to the group.

We can support physical recovery by making smart choices with our eating habits.

Allow the group to process in the information learned about what the body goes through as a result from using.

This last question will give the group a chance to think about what to do, and leads nicely into sharing the information of healthy eating.

Why would nurition matter during recovery?

Alcohol or drug use puts a great deal of stress on the body, proper nutrition will promote healing and improve the odds of staying sober.

Provide group members with handout 10.1 and 10.2

"people become well much quicker, with far fewer symptoms—and stay drug free much longer—when they follow principles of good nutrition" [5]

Discussion Questions:

1. How are you feeling after learning more about your physical recovery?

2. Does your body let you know when it needs nutrients?

3. What foods should we eat to support physical recovery?

4. Where did you learn about healthy eating?

5. Did your family/caretakers eat healthy foods while growing up?

How to Eat Healthy:

Some clients may have never experienced a balanced approach to food based on their different situations in childhood and their exposure to health information.

Refer to Handout 10.3 for some examples of the healthy sources of each category as indicated by the 2015-2020 American Guidelines of how to eat healthy. [6]

Add information to the categories based on Figure 10.3 to support clients in learning more about sources of each food group.

In Recovery, clients will need high nutritional value foods to overcome any depletions or effects of poor nutrition on the body.

As clients share the barriers faced, our role as group facilitators is to use our Motivational Interviewing techniques. We focus on validating the client's experience by writing the barriers up on the board.

Go through each barrier listed on the board, and discuss together how it can be solved.

Only offer your own suggestions if the group truly is unable to think of how to solve the barriers. We want to promote better efficacy within the group for prioritizing physical health.

List out the following on the board with their serving sizes:

Grains (6 ounces):

Dairy (3 cups):

Proteins (5.5 ounces):

Vegetables (2.5 cups):

Fruits (2 cups):

Oils (3 tablespoons)

Ask clients to identify healthy sources of each category, use what you know to fill in any gaps.

1. What barriers do you face in trying to incorporate these foods into your diet?

Write the barriers on the board as clients shout them out.

2. How can we overcome the barriers we listed? (Start with each barrier listed.)

Group Discussion:

(30 minutes)

Now let's pay attention to your exercise habits.

Discussion Questions:

1. When was the last time you participated in any kind of physical movement for the purposes of exercising or relaxing?

2. What kind of activities do you think you enjoy?

3. Have you noticed a correlation between exercising and mood improvement?

4. Why do you think you avoid exercise?

Give group members handout 10.4. This handout has a list of exercises and some goal setting opportunities.

Before you complete the handout review goal setting:

We want to set SMART goals [8]:

S- specific
M- Measurable
A- achievable (or acceptable)
R- realistic
T – time frame

For example: I will walk on the treadmill for 20 minutes, 3 times a week, for the next month.

Instead of: I am going to run for 5 hours every single day no matter what.

You can imagine the likelihood of completing the first goal is much greater than completing the second!

You could consider assigning accountability partners and/or checking back with group members in about a week to see if they completed their goals.

Before we wrap up for today- does anyone want to share their goal(s) with the group?

Closing Statements and Check Out:

(10-15 minutes)

One by one, go around the group and have clients answer the check-out questions.

Pro Tip #4: Write the check-out questions on the board to help the clients remember what is asked.

This group was an introduction to eating and exercise for the building blocks of good physical health. In this group we:

1. Identified current eating patterns and habits.
2. Compared current eating habits to using eating habits.
3. Discussed the toll of use on the body
4. Provided information for what to eat to support recovery.
5. Discussed and overcame the barriers the clients may face in changing eating habits.
6. Supported clients in setting exercise goals.

Check Out Questions:

1. What is one thing you learned today?
2. How will you implement what you learned?
3. Did you meet your goal set out at the beginning of group?
4. What could have been better about group today?

The Body Could be Recovering From:

• Failing to eat: Users may have a suppressed appetite or forget to eat while under the influence.

• Eating poorly: Those who are addicted to drugs or alcohol tend to prioritize their substance abuse over eating properly. As a result, their diets can be poor and lack sustenance. [1]

• Malnourishment: Malnourishment can result from failing to eat consistently over time or from the body's inability to absorb nutrients necessary for biological processes. [1]

• Overeating: Eating too much can lead to obesity and a number of health conditions associated with excess body fat. [1]

• Organ damage: Substance abuse can damage the liver, stomach lining, pancreas, and intestines, all of which contribute to the proper absorption, digestion, and storage of nutrients. [1]

• Immune system damage: Substances such as alcohol and opiates can suppress the immune system and make the user more susceptible to infections and illnesses. [3][4]

• Gastrointestinal disorders: Alcohol can contribute to chronic gastrointestinal tract inflammation, irritable bowel syndrome, leaky gut syndrome, pathogenic bacterial overgrowth, fungal intestinal infections, and acid reflux. [1]

• Hypoglycemia: Low blood sugar can be caused by a lack of sustenance or proper diet. [1]

Effects of Different Substances on the Body

Opiates	• Lead to a lack of enough nutrients and an imbalance of electrolytes (such as sodium, potassium, and chloride) due to withdrawal effects. [7] • Severe Constipation. • Erratic eating behaviors leading to undernutrition.
Alcohol	• Deficiencies are of the B vitamins (B1, B6, and folic acid). A lack of these nutrients causes anemia and nervous system (neurologic) problems. [7] • Liver Damage: The liver removes toxins from harmful substances. [7] • Pancreas Damage: the pancreas regulates blood sugar and the absorption of fat. [7] • Damage to these two organs results in an imbalance of fluids, calories, protein, and electrolytes. [7]
Stimulants	• Reduces appetite, and leads to weight loss and poor nutrition. • Dehydration and electrolyte imbalances. • Difficulty returning to a healthy appetite and diet.
Marijuana	• Marijuana can increase appetite. Some long-term users may be overweight and need to cut back on fat, sugar, and total calories. [7] • Smoking marijuana can seriously effect the lung health.

What's in a Healthy Eating Pattern?

The *2015–2020 Dietary Guidelines* has recommendations for a healthy eating pattern.

For someone who needs 2,000 calories a day, a healthy eating pattern includes:

Fruits, especially whole fruits
2 cups

A variety of vegetables — dark green, red and orange, starchy, legumes (beans and peas), and other vegetables
2½ cups

Fat-free or low-fat dairy, including milk, yogurt, cheese, and/or fortified soy beverages
3 cups

Grains, at least half of which are whole grains
6 ounces

A variety of protein foods, including seafood, lean meats and poultry, eggs, legumes (beans and peas), soy products, and nuts and seeds
5½ ounces

Oils, like canola and olive oil or foods that are sources of oils, like nuts and avocados
5 teaspoons

And it has limits on:

Saturated and *trans* fats — limit saturated fats to less than 10% of daily calories and keep *trans* fat intake as low as possible

Added sugars — limit to less than 10% of daily calories

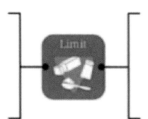

Sodium — limit to less than 2,300 mg a day for adults and children 14 years and up (less for younger children)

[6]

ODPHP | Office of Disease Prevention and Health Promotion   2015 –2020 Dietary Guidelines for Americans — How to Build a Healthy Eating Pattern

Exercises I enjoy or would like to try:

yoga ___	soccer ___	plyometrics ___
kayaking ___	skipping rope ___	brisk walking ___
climbing ___	cycling (outdoor) ___	TRX bands ___
running ___	aerobics ___	hot yoga ___
interval sprints ___	circuit training ___	areial yoga ___
walking ___	hiking ___	cross fit ___
skiing ___	stair-master ___	barre ___
heavy weight lifting ___	spin class ___	trampoline ___
light weight lifting ___	gardening ___	cross-country skiing ___
mat pilates ___	resistance bands ___	tae-kwon-do ___
zumba ___	dog walking ___	surfing ___
salsa dancing ___	kite surfing ___	high intensity interval ___
rowing ___	orange theory ___	other: _____ ___
elliptcal ___	pelaton ___	other: _____ ___
basketball ___	reformer pilates ___	other: _____ ___

My Exercise Goals Are:

(SMART focused)

Sources

1. American Addiction Centers Resource. (2018, December 8). Nutrition and Addiction Recovery. Retrieved September 2019, from: https://www.recovery.org/treatement-therapy/nutrition

2. Miller, R. P. (2010). Nutrition in Addiction Recovery. Many Hands Sustainability Center.

3. Morphine-Induced Immunosuppression, From Brain to Spleen. (2008, June 1). Retrieved September 2019 from: https://archives/drugabuse.gov/news-events/nida-notes/2008/06/morphine-induced-immunosuppression-brain-to-spleen.

4. Drugs, A and HIV (2005, June 21). Retrieved September 2019 from: https//www.hiv.va/gov/patient/daily/alcohol-drugs/immune-system.asp.

5. Finnegan, John. Understanding Oils and Fats. (California: Leysian Arts), 1990 as cited in Finnegan and Gray, 1990.

6. How to Build A Healthy Eating Pattern. Article. (2015). Office of Disease Prevention and Health Promotion.

7. Diet and Substance Abuse Recovery. MedlinePlus website. http://www.nlm.nih.gov/medlineplus/ency/article/002149.htm. Updated March 22, 2013. Accessed September 2019.

8. SMART Recovery: https://www.smartrecovery.org/smart-recovery-toolbox/values-and-goals-clarification/. Accessed March 29, 2020

Three Bonus Ice Breakers

"Ice breakers" are like mini games that get everyone relaxed, playful, and warmed up to interaction.

Whether you are working with a "closed" group, or a group that regularly has members roll in and roll out, creating group cohesion can be an ongoing challenge. Ice breakers are a useful tool for getting group members to relax and to enjoy a natural pleasant interaction with one-another. They are used in all kinds of settings including schools, corporate events, and trainings to get the conversation started. They work best at the beginning of the group before you get to the heavier topics, or they can also be used at the end of the group to fill time and lighten the mood.

Here are three ice breakers that tended to go over pretty well with everyone in my groups:

Ice Breaker #1: Tattoo Talk.

Now a-days, people have tattoos. Lots of them. These tattoos have stories that are personal, hilarious, and/or totally meaningless. Give group members a piece of paper and a pen. Ask them to draw out one of their tattoos. If they do not happen to have a tattoo, ask them to draw out one they would get if they were so inclined. Go around one by one and have group members share the following:

1. Member's Name
2. Tattoo design
3. What does this tattoo mean to you?

Icebreaker #2: Rock, Paper, Scissor Championship.

Rock, paper, scissors is a lifestyle. There exists a World Rock Paper Scissors Association where you can find tournaments, rulebooks, and the opportunity to officially join the association.

Rock paper scissors knows no gender, no socio-economic status, no race, and no strategies for actually improving your skills. This helps make it a mostly fair game for all. This is how it works:

1. Everyone has to create their stage name like in a proper tournament (Example: Robert AKA "The Great Robert" or Susie AKA "The Defeater of All")
2. Everyone stands up.
3. You introduce the players for each round.
4. The first round is two group members engage in a rock-paper-scissor game. The winner of the game stays sanding, the "loser" sits down.

5. Move to the next 2 standing group members and repeat.
6. Keep going until everyone has played once and you have your standing first round champions.
7. Repeat until you have 1 reigning champion.
8. Do your best to draw a trophy on the board, and write the winner's name in the trophy as they are the reigning champion for the remainder of the group.

(Since your group members will ask: yes, you can do best 2/3 in each game depending on the time you have)

Note: If anyone in the group has any limitations for making the "rock" "paper" "scissor" hand signals, you can decide on alternative signals together as a group (or perhaps skip this ice breaker for now).

Make sure to list rules and establish the agreed upon signs for "rock," "paper," and "scissor" prior to beginning the game.

Ice Breaker #3: Sitting down & Talking Charades

This ice-breaker takes the stand-up game of acting out a person or character using no words to a less hyped level by keeping everyone seated and allowing words to be used.

1. Give each group member the name of a well-known celebrity or character.
2. Allow each member to give hints to who they are while the group takes guesses.
3. The group member may use words to describe who they are but cannot tell the group what they are. That means no use of the descriptors "I'm a man, woman, cartoon, character, etc". Examples of what they can say are: lines the character is famous for, sounds the character makes, other descriptors like who they were married to, what they achieved, or where they lived such as "I am best known for living in a pineapple under the sea" (answer: spongebob square pants!)
4. Keep going until everyone has had a chance to play the role of describer.

Some Ideas for celebrities and characters are: Britney Spears, Spongebob Square Pants, Elvis, Ace Ventura, Winnie the Pooh, Gollum, Shrek, Brad Pitt, Justin Bieber, and Yoda.

Made in the USA
Las Vegas, NV
03 May 2024

89474550R00074